POWERLESS

HEALING FROM THE ADDICTION OF A LOVED ONE

2

POWERLESS

Healing from the Addiction of a Loved One

By Anne Jobes

PEN PUBLISHING

Jobes, Anne, 2009
    Powerless, Healing from the Addiction of a Loved One, First Edition, 09 Nov 2009
Includes bibliographical references.
ISBN 978-1449556752 (soft cover), EAN-139781449556754, Book ##3405251

1. Abuse; Heroin; Addiction; Co-dependency; Healing

Copyright April, 2009 by Anne Jobes

LIBRARY OF CONGRESS CATALOGING-IN-PUBLICATION DATA
All rights reserved
No part of this book may be reproduced or utilized in any form or by any means, electronic or mechanical, or by an information storage and retrieval system, without written permission from the author. E-mail Anne Jobes at anne.jobes@yahoo.com

Book cover photography by Judy A. Jones
Special thanks to my daughters Kim and Sydney for their assistance in editing this book, to my son, Conner, for allowing me to share the intimate details of his story, and to my many friends who were kind enough to read my manuscript and offer honest suggestions to me.

Much as we would like, we cannot bring everyone with us on this journey called recovery. We are not being disloyal by allowing ourselves to move forward. We don't have to wait for those we love to decide to change as well.

Sometimes we need to give ourselves permission to grow, even though the people we love are not ready to change. We may even need to leave people behind in their dysfunction or suffering because we cannot recover for them. We don't need to suffer with them.

It doesn't help.

It doesn't help for us to stay stuck just because someone we love is stuck. The potential for helping others is far greater when we detach, work on ourselves, and stop trying to force others to change with us.

Changing ourselves, allowing ourselves to grow while others seek their own path, is how we have the most beneficial impact on people we love. We're accountable for ourselves. They're accountable for themselves. We let them go, and let ourselves grow.

Today, I will affirm that it is my right to grow and change, even though someone I love may not be growing and changing alongside me.

-Melody Beattie

6

Dedicated to my beloved children and to all the mothers of children whose lives have been wounded by addiction.

8

INTRODUCTION

It wasn't always like this. There were so many moments of joy. There were so many precious inspirations of hope.

Bright blue eyes and a devilish smile greeted my mornings. His laughter was contagious. His intelligence and talents were intimidating. He had a boisterous sense of humor. He also embodied a perpetual sweetness, and had a quiet, shyness that was intriguing. Even as a small boy he seemed spiritual in nature - a deep thinker who was compassionate, sensitive, and considerate.

So, how could it have come to this? He had developed into a self-destructive, self-loathing, and tortured soul who clung to his mistakes, and had become blind to his own future. He was unable to hold down a job – unable to pay his own bills. He was a heroin addict – always trying to recover – always trying to stay clean, and constantly succumbing to the fear that put a needle in his arm.

ONE

"Mom, can you come downstairs? I'm down here right now. Bring your cell phone, okay?" He was calling from the lobby of my office building.

At this point, I had gotten tired of his calls. He always wanted money. It was always an emergency. There was always an excuse. I always gave in. For that reason, more than any, I was irritated – I knew I'd give in again.

I got on the elevator and went down the 34 floors to the lobby of my building.

There he was – standing outside in the cold February air with no jacket on. His jeans were sagging. His t-shirt was dirty. His shoes weren't tied. He wore no socks. His hair needed cut, and he smelled as if he hadn't had a shower in days.

I was defensive right away. My finances couldn't take any more pressure. "WHAT do you want, NOW, Conner?"

"Mom, don't get mad," he pleaded. The look of anxiety on his face – the sadness was palpable, and though still impatient, I softened just a little.

"Conner, I know you're here for money, and I just don't have it!"

"I do need money again, Mom. I'm sorry… But, I have to tell you something." He looked nervous.

"What?" I replied.

He looked at me with a desperation that begged for understanding.

"I need help."

Oh, God – I thought – is it a legal issue? Was he in trouble with the law? Had he done something really awful?

"What is it?" I asked reluctantly.

He looked deeply into my eyes, pleading for understanding.

Through tears he said, "I need to go to rehab. I'm addicted to heroin."

For some reason I was not shocked. In one moment everything made sense: the inability to hold down a job, his unkempt posture, the thievery, and the lies. In one fell swoop I realized that it wasn't my bright-eyed little boy who had acted this way – it was an evil demon that had possessed his precious mind, and shrouded his heart.

I was calm – almost relieved.

"Okay," I said, "so what do you need me to do?"

"Can you call Access for me?"

Access Rehabilitation Services in Anderson, Rhode Island was a well-known rehab near Portersville, where we live. I immediately looked up the number, and called them. I spoke with a counselor who asked me a few questions but then let me know that it was Conner who needed to call. I told her that he was standing right beside me, and handed him the phone.

She must have asked him what his "drug of choice" was because he said; "I'm a heroin addict." A tear slid down his cheek.

She asked him a couple more questions. I listened to him answer with a serene kind of hope in my heart. Maybe now the nightmare would end.

Little did I know that it had only just begun.

TWO

When a loved one is abusing drugs, in one way or another, so are you. At least, it was true for me. I wasn't able to separate myself from his addiction. While he waited for an open bed in detox, we waited together. When he needed a fix or two or ten to get through the day, we needed it together. When he missed his appointments because he just didn't bother going when he wasn't dope sick (even though he made-up excuses about it), we missed those appointments together.

And finally, on March 10th – because he didn't have a cell phone of his own – Access Rehabilitation Center called me to tell me that there was an open bed if he could get there before 2pm – I felt like it was my open bed – my opportunity to recover, and leave this part of my life behind me.

I couldn't get in touch with him. He was staying with his girlfriend, Madison – a young girl who (honestly) didn't have a real chance in life. I called Madison's house. No luck. Conner had been down to see me earlier to get money for his daily fix. He had used my cell phone to call his dealer, David. I was so eager to get him into recovery that I actually called David's phone.

"Hi, this is Conner's Mommy – if you see him could you please tell him to call me? You see, there's a bed in rehab if he can get there before 2pm. Thanks."

Had I really made such an incredible fool of myself?

Finally, Conner called. It was 1:30pm. He didn't think he could make it by 2pm – the drive was a 30-minute drive, and he didn't have his "stuff" ready. Little did I know that what he was saying was that he did not intend to go "sick," and needed to shoot more poison in his arm before he made the trip.

I called Access, and begged for an extension on the time. They agreed that as long as he got there before 7pm they'd hold the space for him.

We had packed a small bag previously – awaiting the open bed call. Conner climbed in his car with the suitcase, stopped at my place of work, and by 3:30pm was on his way to Anderson, Rhode Island and a new beginning.

At least that's what I thought.

THREE

I had received a call from Conner's counselor late that evening confirming that he had arrived at Access, and was in detox. For the first time in a long time I slept well that night. I didn't need to worry about where my son was; who he was with, if he was okay – if he was alive. He was safe. He would be in rehab for at least 3-4 weeks. I laid my head down, and slumbered peacefully.

Eleven days later my world crashed down around me.

I was at work – still feeling the relief of my son's immanent recovery. I was beginning to feel less stressed – more hopeful. A woman I work with, Jeannie, casually mentioned that she saw Conner's car over the weekend. She said it was sitting outside of his girlfriend, Madison's house, and that she thought she saw him leaning on it smoking a cigarette.

I argued with her that there was no way she could have seen Conner. But she told me that she was pretty sure she had.

I was confused.

He wasn't supposed to be out of rehab for several weeks.

I had just gone to see him Thursday afternoon. He seemed inspired, committed, and optimistic.

We had walked together outside, and sat with one another across a table in the dining room. He told me all the things he was doing – the activities that were bringing him back to himself.

Why would he have been leaning on his car outside of Madison's house smoking a cigarette?

FOUR

"Simon, Simon and Baker, Law Offices, this is Anne. How may I help you?" I was ill prepared for what I would hear on the other end of the phone or what kind of emotional roller coaster ride I was about to begin.

"Hi, Mom."

"Conner! What are you doing? Where are you? Jeannie said she saw you at Madison's house on Saturday. Why were you at Madison's? Where are you now? Are you still at Madison's? Why aren't you at Access anymore?" I needed answers, and couldn't get the questions out fast enough!

"They fuckin' kicked me out."

"What? WHY?" (No – No – This can't be.)

"They caught me in the stairway with a girl. I tried to stay, but they told me that I had to leave. They wouldn't listen. I should have gotten another chance. Other people there got second chances."

(Oh, okay – so it wasn't HIS fault – it was someone else's).

"Conner, what are you going to do? You're not using, are you?"

"What do you think, Mom? I was only there for ten days. That's not enough time. They really fucked me. They didn't have to kick me out. Now I don't know when I'll be able to get back in."

We went back and forth with his not taking responsibility, and me wanting to "save" him for a while. He told me he was staying with Madison. I gave him Access' number so he might get back in. He said he'd call.

He asked me not to tell his sisters. He was embarrassed – he felt like a failure. I understood.

He begged me not to mention it to his father. I agreed. For the first time in years Sam was feeling a small amount of pride in Conner, and we didn't want to take that away from either one of them.

We hung up.

Aside from Conner's asking, I doubt I would have told Sam anyway. I really didn't want to hear any more screaming or blame or belittling concerning our son.

No matter what choices he had made or what kind of trouble he was in, he was my child first – my beloved child. I knew his heart – I knew his soul, and the connection we had was uncanny. It wasn't that I simply didn't want to hear Sam's condemnation of Conner – I just couldn't hear it any more.

In retrospect I now realize that Sam's demeaning attitude toward Conner was something

I always took very personally. Not only because it questioned my skills as a mother but also (perhaps even more acutely) because it somehow interrogated who I was – my worth.

In addition, I deeply felt Conner's discomfort. I'd lived through abuse myself. I knew the pain that was inflicted by a parent's constant criticism. I knew firsthand the insecurity that was built inside ones heart when everything you are is negated by the person in your life whose love you need the most – by the person you desperately have to trust, and need to feel safe with.

I stood in his shoes, accepted his addiction as an attachment of myself, and agreed to keep his humiliation quiet.

FIVE

I don't know what it was that caused his father to become so impatient with Conner. For the first few years of his life, and through the birth of our daughters, Sam had always seemed to be the ideal dad (at least, from my limited perspective). He spent time with all three kids, played with them, and helped care for them when I was teaching in the evening. He appeared to be a capable and loving father. There was no doubt in my mind that he loved them very much.

However, things were oftentimes angry in our home.

There may have been other incidences (and in hindsight there probably were), but to my recollection, the first one was when Conner was just short of five years old. It was September. His birthday is in January. We were eating breakfast on a Saturday morning. Dippy eggs, bacon, and toast filled our plates. Each child had a glass of milk, and we were talking with one another like we always did.

Then it happened.

Conner moved a little too quickly, and knocked his glass of milk over. What little was left in his cup quickly spread across the tablecloth – a few drops even hitting his father's plate.

"What the Hell are you doing?" Sam screamed. "Can't you be more careful?" He stood up, acting as if the world would surely come to an end – telling Conner that he was clumsy, and that he never did anything right. He called him "stupid." He screamed about wasting money. And when 4-½ year old Conner looked at his father with fear, and confusion, Sam told him to "stop looking at me like that!" and shoved Conner's face into his dippy eggs.

I can still remember the echo of silence that filled the room in those first minutes afterwards. The girls were frightened. They sat silently, mouths gaping open – eyes averting from the upsetting scene in front of them.

I remember feeling shocked – as if I didn't know what to do next, and scared – afraid of my husband's wrath – completely paralyzed with a feeling of uncertainty and trepidation.

Sam sat back down and began to eat angrily as I wiped the table, and my son's face. The rest of the meal was quiet. I don't think any of us could wait to remove ourselves from the discomfort of the situation, put it behind us, and hope it would never happen again.

Had it been a one-time occurrence the memory of it might have faded into the back corners of our hearts rather swiftly, but it was, unfortunately, a moment in time that would be represented weekly for the next twenty years.

SIX

For the rest of that week I heard from Conner almost daily. It wasn't because we were trying to keep in touch, but because he needed money. He'd come down to where I work or he'd meet me in some parking lot somewhere. There was always a fear that his father would see his car, and we acted as if we were on a covert mission – getting him money to buy "popcorn" (a slang name for multiple bags of heroin) from his dealer, David (or whomever else he could find) to provide the needed gear to get high – to stop the withdrawal that would come if he didn't have it.

A couple of times he needed gas money or food, and I'd give him that too. My worst fear was that he'd get shot or overdose while we waited for an open bed again. He said they told him it would likely be a couple of weeks.

Little did I know that he hadn't even called. He already knew that they weren't going to let him come back for at least six months.

SEVEN

One week after he was kicked out of rehab, Sam was going away to an event in Yardley, Rhode Island and I invited Conner to come home – to stay with me in a clean, safe place – even if it was only going to be for a couple of days. We decided that I would pick him up in my car and then drop him off on Sunday so that no one saw his car in front of our house (since he was still supposed to be in recovery).

My oldest daughter, Sydney lived in Canada, and her younger sister, Kim lived far enough away in a city suburb called Seaton Hill with her boyfriend. The coast was clear!

When I picked Conner up we drove to another area of town called Pembrooke. He (we) had to get enough dope to make it through the weekend. Ten bags. I dropped him off, and parked just around the corner (so David didn't see me). I guess dope dealers don't trust strangers.

He got back into the car only a few minutes later.

"Okay," he said.

I found that I was suddenly very curious. What did heroin look like? How was it packaged?

Looking back now I realize that I was trying to share my son's experience with him – I was trying to stay connected.

"Can I see it?"

"What?" Conner asked, "Why? Come on, Mom."

"I just want to see what it looks like."

He pulled a small group of tiny packages out of his pocket. They were wrapped in a small rubber band. They were flat pieces of waxed paper, dime-sized, rectangular packages with a blue stamp on each one.

I was surprised by how small something that sells for $80.00 could be! Good thing you got a discount when you bought in bulk.

We drove home. We discussed how eager he was to use some. I told him that I thought he should hold off as long as possible so that the whole ten bags would last. He explained that it had been nearly four hours since his last fix, and he didn't want to get sick. He seemed almost frightened.

Trying to be practical – and giving him all my best advice (since I was such an expert), I suggested that I hold the dope and give it to him about every 6-8 hours so that he would have enough for the weekend – you know, a constant supply without the worry.

Looking back now, I realize how ridiculous my ideas were. Certainly they were sensible, and very methodical. And since buying poison from a self-interested person who is trying to make an illegal buck on the weaknesses of possessed people, mixing the shit, and putting in your arm is such a logical thing to do – my little plan made all the sense in the world.

NOT!

To anyone else I would have seemed like a blind control freak that was trying desperately to right all that was wrong by trying to create some kind of sanity out of something insane – someone who was not in touch with reality at all.

They would have been right.

At the time I really believed I was guiding my son through an awful ordeal as comfortably as possible.

This was one of the first signs that this was my addiction too.

I just didn't know it yet.

EIGHT

A part of me knew that some of the things I was doing weren't the right things to do. Deep down I was aware that I was somehow supporting his habit – giving him a reason to not take responsibility for his own actions. Yet, in my own mind I was also aware that by enabling him, I was also enabling his aliveness. I was terrified of his being killed or dying.

So I lied about it.

I lied about his still being at Access.

I lied about his on-going recovery.

I lied about where he was, and what he was doing.

I even lied to myself.

I told myself that it was only for a little while – that he would be back in recovery soon – maybe next week – and that all of this would finally be behind us. Only one more week, and then we'd be okay.

We would be okay?

When did it turn into "we?"

Perhaps it was that first moment he was born.

NINE

It was a cold January morning in 1983 at 12:13pm when Conner made his entrance into the world. As my doctor helped him into the room, I watched his arrival with a gratifying sense of amazement! It was surreal! There he was – my little boy – the baby I'd waited excitedly for all those months! My dreams were coming true. My husband and I were suddenly complete.

The first time I held him – when he looked into my eyes – I remember thinking that I'd known him forever. Our bond was immediate, and I loved him with all my heart. I knew, in that moment, that I'd do anything for him – I'd protect him with my life – I'd die for him.

TEN

When we walked into the house Conner immediately headed up the stairs. I followed him with a morbid curiosity. What my son was doing – what I was doing – was preparing to shoot heroin into a vein.

There was a peculiar need at the time to somehow understand the process – what was it one did – how did it work?

Conner knew me well enough – no matter how irritating or embarrassing it probably was – to find his patience with me. I wanted to watch him prepare the deadly liquid for siphon into the syringe. I asked him questions. He answered them.

A bottle cap – a small piece of cotton - a few drops of water – a packet of powder – mix well, draw up.

Tie something tight around your upper arm.

Tap your vein (if there's one left that's not collapsed), and insert needle.

Euphoria!

Conner didn't let me watch beyond the mixing.

I didn't want to.

But when he came out of the bathroom his eyes were glazed over, he was smiling, and he seemed peaceful.

It was odd but I had a sense that for a few hours everything would be fine, and we could just have a nice visit – as if he'd come over for coffee.

ELEVEN

This isn't really a story about Conner and his addiction. It's really about me, and how I became addicted to my son's addiction. It's about how I have begun to let go. It's about survival.

And survival is something I'm pretty good at.

TWELVE

An Unwed Mother's Home is a facility that cares for unmarried women who are pregnant. They provide prenatal care and adoption services in a home-like setting for those outcasts from society who have gotten pregnant out of wedlock. Although there are not many of them in existence any longer, in the early fifties there were two in Portersville. One of them was called Stalle Home.

On July 31st, 1955 at 2:45pm, weighing in at 4 pounds, 14 ounces, I was born in the labor room of an Unwed Mother's Home - backside first. My mother was alone in the room – awaiting the doctor. The nurse had run to get him when she realized that I was coming so quickly.

Moments later I was swept away into an incubator, and off to the nursery. The plan was adoption. I was going to be adopted by another family because my mother, at 30 years old, with only a small income, and no family support, was unable to care for a child on her own.

Nineteen minutes later her plans changed.

My sister, Janet, was born at 3:04pm only hours before our due date. She weighed 6 pounds, 4 ounces, and was mostly unexpected.

About a week before we were born the doctor commented that he thought he heard an "echo" while listening to the baby's heartbeat with a

Fetoscope (an obstetric tool that allowed the doctor to listen to the baby's heartbeat through a stethoscopic device attached to the forehead). He brushed it off though, and my mother didn't really consider the idea of two babies until the arrival of my "younger" sister only minutes after mine.

They whisked Janet away as well, but my mother was left with an overwhelming question: would she have the strength to give up two babies – to have them knowingly separated?

After a time of deliberation over the next few days she decided that she would not be able to give us away – it was twice as hard – and so, at the end of two weeks we went home with her.

Since she had lived at Stalle Home throughout most of her pregnancy the expenses for her care were paid for through the Salvation Army, and the state of Rhode Island. Since she was already a part of the Welfare system she was able to get housing at a project called Clarence Village.

We moved into a small apartment at the end of August, and with some help from a few family members that felt no more than pity for her, she was able to gather a small amount of furniture and a crib (which Janet and I shared for several months until she was able to attain a second one).

Naturally, I don't recall any of those first few years, but from what I was told; my maternal grandmother spent a good amount of time there helping with baby care in those early days.

She attached herself to me.

She was openly hesitant to spend time with Janet because (as we found out later), Janet looked too much like my mother, and my grandmother didn't really like my mother.

Perhaps that is the reason things turned out for me the way they did – at least, partially: my grandmother's disdain for my mother, my mother's jealousy of her own mother's attention to me, and the empathy she felt for my sister.

Psychology is a fascinating study. We are so deeply affected by, not only our circumstances, but by the conditions of everyone around us. It's a captivating web of connection, and confusion – a tapestry of personality, insecurity, and power. It embraced me, shrouded me, and wove its spiny fingers through my heart.

Fortunately, it only served to strengthen my Soul.

THIRTEEN

A few hours went by. Conner and I talked a little. At this point I was desperate to understand what it was that he was going through – why it had been so easy to slip back into using after he'd been clean for a whole ten days (which, at the time, I actually thought was long enough)! I kept thinking that if he wanted to quit – although I'm sure it was difficult – all he had to do was put his mind to it, and he could just stop using. I mean – it was awful stuff – deadly…it made him sick…distanced him from everyone that he loved. He said he wanted to be clean.

Why was he using then?

What I didn't understand at that point was that *the human brain is an extraordinarily complex and fine-tuned communications network containing billions of specialized cells (called neurons) that give origin to our thoughts, emotions, perceptions and drives. Often, a drug is taken the first time by choice to feel pleasure or to relieve depression or stress. But this notion of choice is short-lived because repeated drug use disrupts well-balanced systems in the human brain in ways that persist, eventually replacing a person's normal needs and desires with a one-track mission to seek and use drugs. At this point, normal desires and motives will have a hard time competing with the desire to take a drug.*[1]

That evening, although I didn't understand any of the facts yet, I began to understand how truly out of Conner's own control he really was.

About four hours after his last "hit," he started getting antsy. He asked me for another bag. It was still only Friday evening, and I knew that if he kept using at this pace he'd never make it through the weekend with the nine bags he had left. One of my major concerns was that he'd want more money, and I didn't have it. The stress of continually coming up with cash was really nerve-racking, and combined with my constant concern for Conner; I knew it had to be affecting my health and well being adversely.

So, I tried to hold him off. I asked him to wait another hour.

He started to act very nervous. He tried to explain to me that he was going to start getting sick. He told me his nose was already starting to run. He didn't want to be sick. He said it over, and over again. And naturally, I eventually gave in.

"I'll be right back."

---

[1] Nora D. Volkow, M.D., Addiction and the Brain's Pleasure Pathway: Beyond Willpower

Off he went – upstairs to mix, stir, and shoot again.

I felt almost numb with fear.

I felt out of control.

I felt tired.

I heard him coming down the steps. I expected to see that glazed-over look in his eyes that told me he'd be happy and comfortable for the next few hours.

Instead, he looked frightened and angry.

"What's wrong?" I asked.

"My needle broke. I can't get it fixed. Does Dad have any?"

"What?" (Does Dad have any?) "No, he wouldn't have anything like that. What do you mean your needle broke?"

"The plunger – it's stuck inside, and I can't get it out." He was beginning to act panicky.

"Well, can't you just snort it then?" It seemed reasonable to me. That's what he used to do before he began mainlining…it should work, right? (Am I out of my mind?)

"NO, Mom! You don't understand! That won't work! It won't be enough! Now that I've been shooting it won't work the same way! I'll have to use more of it! What I have won't even last through tomorrow! I HAVE to find another needle!"

I suppose it was the fear that struck me the most. He was literally terrified! It was as if he were a wild animal suddenly caged – an animal that felt threatened, and was about to attack!

I tried to calm him, but the more he realized his dilemma, the more panic stricken he became. He did everything he could think of to repair the plunger but when he ran out of ideas he turned to me and asked if I'd drive him somewhere to get a needle.

"Where? Can't we wait until tomorrow?" I felt so confused.

"NO, Mom…NO…we have to get it now. I'm gonna get sick. SHIT! I have to get a needle!" He was pacing. He pounded his fist into the door.

I didn't know what to do.

"Where can you get a needle?"

"I don't know," he said thinking. "Maybe Mike." He started to dial the phone. He tried several people he knew. Then he called a friend of a friend of a friend who said that he might have one – to stop by.

We drove up to the guy's house, but when he saw me he refused to give Conner anything. I guess he thought it was some kind of undercover sting.

When Conner got back in the car he was more frightened than ever! He kept saying, "Mom, I have to find a needle. I'm going to get sick. My legs are starting to cramp. I have to get a needle."

It was awful seeing him like that. I felt myself wanting to find a needle for him so he'd be okay again. Some part of me needed the needle now too.

Finally, he got in touch with Madison who (for $10.00 of my money) said she'd sell him one of her needles. What a nice girl.

We drove to her house, got the needle, and drove home.

He cleaned it out with Clorox – explaining to me that it was necessary to do that so that he didn't pick up any diseases like AIDS or *Hepatitis C*[2] (which he had unknowingly already acquired).

---

[2] **Hepatitis C** is a liver disease caused by the hepatitis C virus (HCV). HCV infection sometimes results in an acute illness, but most often becomes a chronic condition that can lead to cirrhosis of the liver and liver cancer.

Although he was still eager to have his fix he seemed to have calmed down quite a bit now that he would be able to.

Once the needle was clean, he took care of business, and all was (once again) right with the world for the next few hours.

The weekend was a mix of calm confusion and an abnormal kind of gratitude. Sunday morning I took him back to Madison's father's apartment, and went home knowing I had to pretend the weekend hadn't happened the way it had – keeping all of my feelings, concerns and uncertainty to myself.

Transmission: Contact with the blood of an infected person, primarily through sharing contaminated needles to inject drugs. **Vaccination:** There is no vaccine for hepatitis C., Centers for Disease Control and Prevention

FOURTEEN

Growing up was difficult but I didn't really pay attention most of the time. I tucked the bad stuff somewhere deep in some corner of my heart and memory, choosing to stay optimistic. It was as if I couldn't see the negative things. I only paid attention to the comfortable, fun or promising moments.

Songs like, "High Hopes," and "Cock-eyed Optimist" became my personal theme songs. I really allowed myself to see life as a hopeful, positive experience. I believed what Mr. Rogers told me – that I was "special."

But beneath the sunshine there was an emotional tempest brewing.

The details of my childhood are fraught with poverty, anger, jealousy, betrayal, and abuse. Nothing I ever did was good enough. I was a disappointment. I was the "bad" one (Janet being the "good" one). I have so many memories of beatings with the *cat-of-nine-tails*[3] it's not even possible to count them. I've been called every negative name one might imagine. And there were so many disappointments – so many dreams dashed by criticism. My mother was so filled with self-loathing she was unable to truly see what she

---

[3] A whip with nine separate woven tails with a knot and three strands at the end of each one.

was doing. I believe this to be true. The tolerance she had for my sister simply represented the patience and love she wished had been given to her.

One of the more specific memories that stands out in my reminiscence (a little more than some of the others) occurred when I was about twelve years old. I was in my bedroom – I spent a lot of time by myself – listening to my Beatle's albums and fantasizing about being in England – being a personal friend of the fab four.

I heard my mother's voice. She was calling with that irritated, angry voice, and I knew I was in trouble again – I just didn't know what I'd done this time.

I went to the top of the steps.

The house we rented was a small, four-room row house set on an alley often termed "bed bug row." The stairs were dark and steep. Looking down the narrow hallway that surrounded the steps I saw my mother's angry face, and my sister, Janet, standing behind her with a smug look on her face.

"What, Mommy?" I asked. I loved her so much. I so very much wanted her to love me.

"Come down here!" she said angrily.

I always felt a little frightened. If she was yelling, there was going to be hitting. I don't know which one was worse, but the combination was always difficult to bear – and it happened all the time. It made me feel unloved – worse – unlovable. I always had the feeling that everything I did was wrong. I was always trying to fix it - to be a good girl - then maybe the beatings, the yelling and the abuse would stop. (It was my fault she got so angry)...

I slowly moved down the steps toward her. "What did I do?" I asked. She stood at the bottom of the steps – her cigarette smoldering – puffs of smoke exiting her mouth as she screamed, "Just get down here!"

I stood on the second step from the bottom, my hand on the railing. I couldn't move any further down because her stance was so aggressively near to me that it would have been impossible to move down to the next step.

"What?" I asked in a quiet, questioning, and cautious voice.

She gritted her teeth. Her dull, green eyes shot daggers at my blue ones. She leaned closer to my face, and with a disgust I cannot describe she said, "I hate you." As she finished the last word, she turned her cigarette onto my arm, and burned me with its blistering flame.

Strange – I don't recall the pain. I don't remember pulling my arm away (if I did). It was as if the physical discomfort was so deeply outweighed by the emotional, that my skin was numb. I felt confused. I weakly asked, "Why?" with tears in my eyes.

"Because you're so ugly!"

I looked into her angry eyes as she pulled away, and just behind her was my sister with a self-satisfied smile on her face.

FIFTEEN

After that weekend with Conner I began to realize that I didn't know enough about heroin addiction.

I suppose I believed that it was like cigarette smoking but bigger. Until my son was the addict, I thought of it as something dirty – something that the lowliest people might do. I had always thought of heroin addicts as thieving liars who would murder if necessary to get high. I knew that it was a drug that controlled a person's mind, and habits, but I guess I still believed that there was some kind of conscious choice involved.

"Alcohol will kill you at 5MPH. Heroin will kill you at 90." My son was killing himself.

I began to do a lot of research. I purchased books, read articles, and I even joined an on-line message board. To date, the books I've read or specials I've watched on television are innumerable!

For me, however, the most helpful information concerning addiction came from HBO. They had done a special four-part series called, "Addiction – Why Can't They Just Stop," and especially after watching the special, and reading the associated book, I felt that I had really begun to grasp what might be going on with my son.

According to Dr. Nora Volkow, *"Addiction is a chronic brain disorder. People who are addicted cannot control their need for alcohol or other drugs, even in the face of negative health, social or legal consequences. This lack of control is the result of drug-induced changes in the brain. Those changes, in turn, cause behavior changes.*
The brains of addicted people "have been modified by the drug in such a way that absence of the drug makes a signal to their brain that is equivalent to the signal of when you are starving". It is "as if the individual was in a state of deprivation, where taking the drug is indispensable for survival. It's as powerful as that."[4]

Once I started to research addiction, I began to realize that what led to my son's overuse of drugs (attempting to blanket his inner pain) was also what probably brought him to his dependence on them. What makes one person abuse drugs to the point of losing their home, their family and their job, while another does not? There is no one simple reason. *Drug abuse and addiction is due to many factors. A powerful force in addiction is the inability to self- soothe or get relief from untreated mental or physical pain. Without the self-resilience and support to handle stress, loneliness or depression, drugs can be a tempting way to deal with the situation. Unfortunately, due to the changes drugs make to the brain, it can only take*

---

[4] Nora D. Volkow, M.D., Understanding Addiction, What Is Addiction?

a few times or even one time to be on the road to addiction.[5]

I also began to see that my son's physiology had been altered over the course of several years – probably since before he ever thought he'd use a drug like heroin.

In addition I realized that the combination of psychological aspects, physical disorders, emotional abuse, as well as the alternations in his brain, and its ability to formulate choices were going to make his recovery a much steeper, up-hill battle than I had originally thought.

Little did I know that my addiction to his recovery was only embryonic.

---

[5] HelpGuide.org, Drug Abuse and Addiction, Signs, Symptoms, Effects and What You Can Do

SIXTEEN

Conner was never very strong or coordinated when it came to any kind of sports. He tried basketball, swimming, and karate for quite some time. He did well, but he just didn't seem to have a natural flare for any of it. It was as if he didn't have the energy to be bothered.

We encouraged him, but each time he'd do poorly, his father would let him know that he was "lazy" and his negative self-image would be cultivated even more. It probably didn't help that Sydney seemed so good at everything she did. She was Daddy's little Princess. She was coordinated and hard working. Conner wasn't.

But Conner was extremely creative. His intelligence was tempered by a genuine compassion. He couldn't do a perfect Kumate' Kata, but he could read a book, and understand the characters, story line, and conclusions better than most adults.

He was an intellectual person who was expected to be "all boy" (whatever that means), and without the ability to run better than next-to-last-place on the Track Team – he was just a loser in his father's eyes. Sam stopped going to the Cross-Country races at the High School after the first poor showing because he didn't want to be embarrassed. He never let Conner forget what a disappointment he was.

Since this was an on-going thread throughout Conner's childhood, I had naturally grown closer to Conner on a different level than I had with the girls.

I had a deep empathy for what Conner was probably feeling. I also knew how important it was that Conner was aware that his father loved him. I continually tried to explain to Conner that his father only said these things because he cared so much and wanted the best for him. "He just doesn't express himself very lovingly, Sweetie," I would say, "But he loves you more than anything."

I don't know if I really believed all of that at the time. I was still struggling with my own feelings of insecurity from the way my mother had treated me. I was still very unsure of her love (and of my loveableness). How could I convince my son that his father loved him when my deepest heart had no proof of it?

I'm sure I didn't come off as being very convincing. That, in-and-of-itself probably created a wider hole in Conner's heart. He probably thought I was lying to him. Because Sam was hard on Conner – I was easy on him.

Because Sam found so much wrong with Conner - I found excuses for his limitations.

Because Sam called him names - I cuddled him, and showed him as much love as possible.

Because Sam got angrier than he needed to when Conner didn't do his best – I let him get away with too much.

Between my husband and me we eventually told Conner that he was worthless, and didn't need to take responsibly for anything – that someone else would do it for him, and that he'd never succeed anyway.

The last thing any child needs is exactly what we gave him.

SEVENTEEN

Two weeks after his expulsion from Access, and one week after the weekend Conner spent at home I became quite upset that we hadn't received word of an open bed yet.

Although Conner didn't have a cell phone, Madison's father did. It was there that I would usually be able to call him or he could call me.

I continued to give him cash almost every day. It averaged about $50 a day, and so by the end of this two-week period I had given him most of any of the money I had in my accounts. This was an obvious case of enabling – but for me it was still about trying to save him: saving him from drug dealers that might shoot him if he cheated them out of the full amount, saving him from going to jail because he was stealing things, saving him because then he'd feel loved, saving him so he wouldn't do something horrible to himself, saving him because – because – because.

It's actually a very "normal" reaction to addiction. Family members become codependent with their addict. They love them. They fear for them. They hold out hope that they can make a difference in the addict's life – help them to stop. Enabling is born in the very unique denial that comes from loving an addict.

Unfortunately, I understood all of that only in theory. My son was different. My son needed me because he had issues that were extenuating. My son was far too volatile to leave him alone in a world full of wolves. My son...

"Many times when family and friends try to "help" addicts, they are actually making it easier for them to continue in the progression of the addiction.

This baffling phenomenon is called "enabling," which takes many forms, all of which have the same effect -- allowing the addict to avoid the consequences of his actions. This in turn allows the addict to continue merrily along his drugging ways, secure in the knowledge that no matter how much he screws up, somebody will always be there to rescue him from his mistakes.

What is the difference between "helping" and "enabling?"

Helping is doing something for someone that they are not capable of doing themselves. Enabling is doing for someone things that they could, and should be doing themselves.

Simply, enabling creates an atmosphere in which the addict can comfortably continue his unacceptable behavior."[6]

---

[6] The Good Shepherd Restoration Ministries, Inc., Enabling

So, when Access hadn't called, and I was losing sleep (and money) every day, I finally got to a point where I had to confront Conner about it.

"How are you, honey? Are you okay?"

"Not really. I wish I was dead. Mom, do you have any money for me today?"

"I'll see…maybe…. Conner, has Access called yet? I don't understand why it's taking so long." I tried to steer the conversation to recovery – after all, I was feeling sick.

"I'm not going back there, Mom. They don't care about me. They only care about money. If they cared they wouldn't have kicked me out to begin with over something so stupid."

"They told you they'd let you come back, right?" He had lied to me so many times – and he did it so well – I was just trying to figure out what was really going on.

"Yeah, they did, but maybe I shouldn't go back there. Maybe I should go somewhere else."

(Maybe I shouldn't go back there? Maybe they won't allow him to go back there).

"Let me call you back, Conner," I said. "I'll do some research – see what's out there. If I find something, do you want to go? I mean, what if they can take you right away?"

"I don't have any gas money. Can I come down and get some money for gas, and stuff?"

(Stuff – what about recovery?)

"Yes. Call me when you're downstairs. I can't give you much, Conner."

"But it'll be enough, right – I mean, only $60 or $70 wouldn't be that much, right?"
($60 or $70? I'm already overdrawn)!

"I don't know what I can give you, but I'll do the best I can."

"Well, if it's not going to be at least $80.00 I may as well not come down. I may as well just slam my car into a brick wall. NEVERMIND, Mom – you JUST DON'T UNDERSTAND!!! Maybe I should just kill myself!"

Okay, so maybe I didn't understand, but his control of my emotions always worked, and he knew it. Addicts are incredible manipulators. My fear that something awful was going to happen to him – my guilt that his father and I didn't do the best job we could have with him – all of these things created a space where I said, "I'll give you $80.00 plus gas money. Just come down. Drive carefully. I'll call a couple of places and let you know."

EIGHTEEN

I hung up with Conner, and immediately called Susan. She had been my original contact at Access Rehabilitation Services the day Conner told me that he was addicted to heroin. She was also the person who had called to confirm with me that he had been admitted to detox. Perhaps she could give me some answers as to why Conner hadn't been offered a bed yet.

After reminding her who I was (I can only imagine how many patients she speaks to daily – let alone their family members), I asked her, "Do you think there'll be a bed for Conner soon? Is there anyone else I should contact?"

She paused for a moment. Then she said, "Anne, Conner won't be allowed to come back to Access for at least six months – not until September."

"What? Why?" I felt the blow as if someone had struck me in the face.

"He broke rules. We are state subsidized. We have to follow protocol."

(Protocol? Isn't protocol helping people recover? So, he fooled around on the stairwell with a female patient. There are worse things, right?)

"Susan, isn't there something we can do? I don't know if he's going to live until September."

"There really isn't. You could call another facility. But it would be Conner that has to call. I mean, he has to take this seriously or it's not going to work. Most heroin addicts end up in rehab at least three times before it really begins to work. You CAN'T do it for him!"

(I know. I know.)

"Who should I call?" I asked. I felt so defeated – disappointed – scared.

Susan gave me names and phone numbers of several other rehab centers in the state. She wished me luck.

Before I got off I had to ask, "He did more than fool around with a female patient on the stairwell, didn't he?"

"Yes."

NINETEEN

Throughout most of our growing years my sister and I were close on quite a few levels. Although Janet betrayed me with my mother many times, we were twins – comrades in life, and shared a history in a household that could be described as "dysfunctional" in many ways. We had a lot of fun together most of the time, and although I didn't trust her completely, I wanted to.

But by the time I began Junior High School I had become less connected with my sister. Her interests had changed. She was incredibly embarrassed about our financial deficiencies. We lived on an alley. We wore hand-me-down clothing. We got one pair of shoes a year – and never any boots in the winter. Our hair wasn't professionally cut. Our mother was not educated. Our father was an ex-con. Janet was mortified to bring anyone to our house.

For some reason, I felt a strange kind of pride in all of that! For me, it was as if I was even more special because I was poor. I knew I was just as important as the more fortunate kids who lived "up the hill" (which, for us, was where the more affluent families resided).

But being poor does a couple of things – at least it did for us. My mother wasn't big on hygiene – which meant we didn't go to the dentist. Our mouths were full of cavities – which made our breath smell. We weren't really encouraged to bathe daily. My stepfather took a bath – literally – only on Saturday night. Although we probably bathed most days, we certainly didn't wash our hair often. It was greasy, and we probably smelled.

We didn't have the convenience of an automatic washing machine. But it wouldn't have mattered. By the time I was in eighth grade I only owned two dresses, and I wore them every other day to school for the whole school year.

Janet was a little more fortunate because by eighth grade she had made friends with a couple of girls who were the same age as us, but much taller. Since this was so, she was able to wear their hand-me-downs from the year before, which were still fashionable. By the time I fit into them (since I was at least two sizes smaller than Janet) they were much worn, and my mother just threw them out.

So, I wore my two dresses.

One can imagine how critical the other kids were. They teased me horribly. I remember being the last one chosen for everything: any team in Phys Ed class, spelling bee lineups – even in Home Ec class.

It was disheartening, and I was embarrassed, ashamed, and lonely.

Still, I remember there being within me a tiny flame of confidence. It was as if I was hurt by my circumstances, and the cruelty of some of the people around me but I was inwardly always aware of my uniqueness, and my genuine ability to care. I always liked whom I was inside. It helped get me through what everyone else seemed to see on the outside.

TWENTY

"Just what makes that silly old ant think he can move that rubber tree plant? Anyone knows an ant can't move a rubber tree plant. But he's got high hopes. He's got high hopes. He's got high apple pie in the sky hopes."[7]

    I have always been a spiritual person. I don't know if I was religious. I always believed in God. I always thought that we had a purpose in life. I always thought that I had a purpose in life – I was more than my mother said – more than the kids at Doramer Junior High School said.

    A couple of friendless years at school created a space in me that allowed me to find empathy. I felt other people's discomfort. I knew that I could make a difference. If I couldn't change my circumstances, maybe I'd change theirs.

---

4 Music by Jimmy Van Heusen, Lyrics by Sammy Cahn

TWENTY-ONE

In ninth grade a young lady came to our school halfway through the year that was one of the homeliest girls I've ever seen. She was chubby, had acne, and oily, stringy hair. She wore old-fashioned clothing, and she smelled of B.O.

Everyone teased her to the point of making her cry.

I befriended her.

In twelfth grade another girl we went to school with, who was actually very pretty (but completely controlled by her parents and teased because of her wardrobe) was always alone. No one seemed to want to spend any time with her.

I befriended her.

I ended up hanging out with all the misfits. I actually liked everyone. I knew that we all had something that was worth liking, and that it wasn't fair to look at someone because of their physical appearance or clothing – where they lived, or what their circumstances were. I suppose it was a very "Christian" way of being – but it was my way.

In retrospect, I think it was my way of feeling special – of feeling good, good about me, and who I was. I was simply trying to counterbalance what I was being told at home. I was trying to be everything my mother told me I wasn't.

And it worked! It felt good to assist others. I felt necessary. I was a much happier person because of it.

As I got older, I continued to do "good" things.

I put money into *C.A.R.E.* Foundation boxes.[8]

I deposited money into people's accounts (secretly) that I worked with if they seemed to need it.

I "adopted" a young girl from India through Christian Children's Fund.

Everything that I did that seemed like I was righting the wrongs of the world (or just one person's life) made me feel happy. It felt "good." I felt as if I was needed.

It was a far cry from the kind of feedback I got when I was at home.

---

[8] A leading humanitarian organization fighting global poverty.

TWENTY-TWO

"The Goser Center", "Emerald Hall", "Bay Run", "Living Clean", and "Rosy Glenn"…

How was I supposed to know which one would be best? I'd heard of "Access" and "The Goser Center" prior to Conner's addiction. Perhaps I could call "The Goser Center".

"No beds."

Okay, so what about, "Living Clean" – that sounded good?

"Detox only – no smoking – if we can get him a bed for rehab afterwards we will, but there are no promises…"

Now what?

Okay, next "Bay Run"…

"Bay Run admissions, this is Sally."

"Hello, Sally… My name is… My son…" (God, how did this happen?)

"If he has a Welfare reference number we can get pick him up, and admit him today."

"Yes, yes…. he has a number. I don't know what it is…but he has one…."

"Have Conner give us a call."

TODAY!

My heart was racing! Today! They'll pick him up! He'll be in detox again by sundown!

When I spoke with Conner he was very open to it. He called Sally back. He told me that they were picking him up in an hour.

An hour!

"What about your car? Do you have your clothes – your suitcases?"

"Madison's father borrowed the car to go to a doctor's appointment. He's not home yet. I don't know. My stuff is mostly in the trunk. I guess I'll have to leave it here."

SHIT!

"Okay, I'll call Madison or her Dad later – tomorrow – and we'll get over there to get your stuff. Call me when the driver comes, okay?"

"Okay, Mom."

"I love you, Conner. I'm so proud of you."

"I love you too, Mom."

TWENTY-THREE

Sam didn't know that Conner had been back on the streets for 18 days. Perhaps he would never know. All I had to do was go over to Madison's father's house, get Conner's stuff, move the car (somewhere) so it would be safe, and not get a ticket while he was in rehab, and sit back.

That's all I had to do!

After several phone calls, I finally decided to drive the car to the Vanderbilt Municipal Building (near Madison's father's house), and park it in their parking lot – with a temporary permit, of course. The officer had told me where to park it, where to put the keys, and the money.

I went over to Madison's father's house with my youngest daughter, Kim and her boyfriend, Aaron. Kim would drive my car a few blocks to the Municipal Building while I drove Conner's.

When we arrived at Jason's (Madison's father) house, my son's car was nowhere to be found.

I knocked on the door. Madison's sister's boyfriend, Josh (also a heroin addict) answered the door. I asked where the car was. "I don't know. I think Madison took it to get a new tire. The tire was flat. She went to get a new one."

"Where is she?"

"I don't know… Dad, do you know where Madison is?"

GODDAMN!

"Can we call her?"

"I don't know…Dad, do you know where Madison is so we can call her about Conner's car?"

(This can't be happening!)

After about ten minutes I was given a number to call Madison. She answered right away, "Hello?"

"Madison, this is Mrs. Jobes. Where is Conner's car?"

"Oh, Hi, Anne. Well, I ummm… I tried to get a new tire for it because the donut was flat, but the wheel didn't fit… It broke down on the side of the road… I left it there, and got a ride from my cousin."

"Madison, where is the car?"

"Just off the road by the Pembrooke exit." Short pause. "I have to get off now, though, because I'm at my cousins birthday party."

I was pissed!

"What do you mean it's on the side of the road?"

"Don't yell at me! It's not my fault it broke down!" And she hung up on me.

There are no words to explain how angry and frustrated I was!

I collected as many pieces of Conner's clothing as I could from Josh – who despite being high was very nice – and we drove to the Pembrooke exit to see what could be done about Conner's car.

By this time it was getting dark. What was supposed to be a one-hour trip was turning into an entire evening!

It was a chilly October twilight. Cars were zipping by us at 60 MPH. I took a look at the tire, and realized there was no way to drive the car all the way to Vanderbilt. Opening the trunk, I gathered more of Conner's things to be sent to Bay Run, and threw away anything that I considered to belong to Madison's family. Debris was collected in a trash bag.

There was a wheel in the trunk with a tire on it. I wondered if we'd be able to change it. I had never done that kind of thing before.

What were my choices? I could change the tire myself (I don't think so); call AAA or maybe a friend?

After a couple of calls (and no luck), I decided to call my nephew, Nate, who didn't live far from the Pembrooke exit. He'd probably be uncomfortable with the reason this happened, but he'd probably be kind about it too.

After a short time he and his wife showed up.

He took one look at the wheel, and told me that he'd be unable to trade wheels because the one in the trunk wasn't the right size for Conner's car.

SHIT!

We stood in the chilly night air in a little semi-circle just staring at Conner's car. I felt like I owed Nate and Caitlin some kind of explanation for asking them to come out to help me like this. I knew how strange it much seem.

"Thank you so much for coming out here tonight to help."

"No problem," Nate said. The look on Caitlin's face seemed to be expressing the need to understand what was going on.

"Conner's girlfriend stole the car, and then left it when it broke down." (What kind of girlfriend does he have? Why is he with someone like that?) I could see it in their eyes…

"Conner's has had some problems with drugs. He's in rehab right now. We were going to move his car, but Madison took it…"

"Oh…"

"Well, thanks for coming. I can't thank you enough!"

And they left.

Turning to Kim I said, "We're going to have to call AAA."

An hour later Conner's car was safely parked at the Vanderbilt Municipal Building, and we were on our way home.

TWENTY-FOUR

I met Sam on the first day of school my senior year. I disliked him immeasurably within the first few minutes of class. I thought he was ignorant, self-serving, and mean. He made fun of other people in the room (including the teacher). It was obvious this was Mr. Peters first year as a teacher, and that he was very nervous. Sam relentlessly badgered him to his face! I don't think Mr. Peters knew what to do, exactly. I felt sorry for him.

Sam's whole attitude was pompous. He laughed louder than anyone else in the room (on purpose), and didn't represent just the "class clown," but the class narcissist. It was all about him. The whole room paid him an enormous amount of attention. He was funny (in a cruel way), and the world was his audience!

I was (at that point in my life) a bit of a flower child - a "Jesus freak" – still in Girl Scouts (and proud of it!). I played the guitar, and sang folk songs. I always volunteered for the Muscular Dystrophy Association. I didn't swear. I didn't drink. I didn't use drugs. I was "high on life," and his kind of negativism really turned me off. I had befriended every "freak" in school, and felt a deep level of caring for every person I met.

Still, I couldn't shake my distaste for Sam. I didn't realize it at the time, but I probably didn't like him because he reminded me of my mother.

She, too, was disrespectful, callous, and self-interested.

I would later discover that it was probably the qualities they had in common that almost certainly attracted me to him. My mother's abuse and emotional abandonment had left a wide hole in my heart. The psychology is fascinating! No doubt I connected with someone similar to her - he was so familiar – whom I was comfortable with (used to), but also in whom I might find restitution. If I could make him love me, then in some ass-backwards way, I was making my mother love me. Of course, this breakthrough in awareness of my behavior didn't come until at least 35 years after I met Sam. Until then, I had to figure out how to deal with him!

The feeling of dread was so terrible that on the third morning of school I made an appointment to speak with my school counselor so I might switch my math class. I didn't think I could stand being in the same room with him for a whole school year!
Unfortunately Mrs. Miller told me that there were no other classes 7th period that I could move to, and told me to just "stick it out."

I walked into my 7th period class on that third day of school completely anxious about the next 45 minutes!

Then along came Dane Henkley.

Dane was a tall, rather good-looking (in a puppy dog kind of way) boy in my class who didn't seem to understand Magic Squares at all! *A Magic Square is a square that contains numbers arranged in equal rows and columns such that the sum of each row, column, and sometimes diagonal is the same.*[9]

As we worked on the puzzle, Dane kept turning around and asking if anyone could help him. Finally, I decided that the best way for Dane to do the puzzle was for someone to explain it to him. Naturally, I took on the task with enthusiasm! Not only did I believe that we should help one another – let's face it – it made me feel capable, special, and smart.

An interesting side-note on what I've learned about myself over the years has got to be how honest I've become concerning my "intent" in helping others. It's not that there's anything wrong with helping, but as I've come to find out – I'm not so much a helper in most cases as I am an enabler. And either way – the bottom line – I might just be doing it for me more than anyone else (but that's a whole other book).

Anyway, after helping Dane figure out how to do a Magic Square I decided that if I could have a "purpose" in Applied Math class it might just be to help Dane, and maybe by helping Dane I

---

[9] The Free Dictionary by FARLEX

would be able to find a way to put up with Sam (who certainly was difficult to ignore)!

TWENTY-FIVE

Most addiction treatments are designed to do more than simply reduce or remove alcohol or drug use - they focus on getting addicted people to change their lifestyle and even their core life values as a way of preventing return of the problems. Like treatments for other conditions, addiction treatments can also include medications and forms of talk therapy, but addiction treatments may be provided by a much wider range of personnel (clergy, counselors, social workers, physicians) than most other forms of healthcare.[10]

Conner was in Bay Run for three full weeks. He had gone through the detoxification and stabilization part of his treatment where they had rid his body of any immediate traces of heroin (or other drugs).

While he was in the rehabilitation part of care he saw a depression counselor, and well as a drug counselor. He was given blood tests again to confirm whether he had acquired Hepatitis C or AIDS. He was eating regular, healthy meals, and attending in-house N.A. meetings.

He called me as often as he could. He seemed to move in and out of a state of sadness or happiness, but definitely seemed to be responding

---

[10] A. Thomas McLellan, Ph.D, Addiction, What is Addiction Treatment

well to the therapy that Bay Run Behavioral Health System was providing, and told us that the setting was really nice.

    He told me about friends he was making – walks by the river – the trees and surrounding area – and (eventually) how much he really wanted to stay clean. He believed in his own strength, and I could hear a confidence in his voice that I hadn't heard for a very long time (if ever).

    Those three weeks when he was in Bay Run were wonderful for me. I felt calm, grateful, optimistic, and well rested. The house was quiet, and although I was still wondering if I'd ever recover from the financial strain of Conner's (my) addiction, I felt hopeful.

    It was a peaceful three weeks.

TWENTY-SIX

I received a call from Conner on Tuesday, April 30th. He was calling from his counselor's office.

We had hashed out the idea of his going to a halfway house after rehab several times over the course of the last week so I was not sure how I felt when Conner announced,
"I'm coming home tomorrow."

"Tomorrow?" (Fear) "Are you sure you're ready?"

"I'm fine, Mom. I feel really good. Can you pick me up – they have to drop me off on the North Side at the Bay Run office there?"

"Of course I can. What time?" I was terrified!

"I don't know. We'll probably leave here in the morning after breakfast. It'll be a couple of hours. I can call you when I get there."

"Okay – I'll drive in to work tomorrow, and then take my lunch hour to pick you up. Maybe I'll take half a day off." (Is he really ready?)

"Okay, Mom – see you tomorrow!"

I hung up.

He was coming home tomorrow. He sounded really good. I was hopeful. I was also petrified! What if he needed more time? Should he have gone to a halfway house? Now what happens?

I called Sam and the girls.

"Conner will be home tomorrow!" I tried to sound as hopeful as possible.

TWENTY-SEVEN

"Mom, my knee hurts."

I had learned not to make too big a deal of the kid's complaints. My rule of thumb was, "if there ain't blood, don't worry about it." It isn't that I was insensitive. I ran a family day care in my home, and when you looked after between four and eight children daily, you simply learned not to sweat the little stuff.

"It's probably just sore from running, Honey." (Conner was attempting Cross Country running for the High School at the time). "I'm sure it'll be just fine in a few days.

He told me it hurt again in about two weeks. This time he reported swelling.

I still blew it off as (perhaps) a reason to quit the Cross Country team. Conner wasn't a natural runner, and he kept coming in almost last. It didn't make him feel very good about himself.

Another month went by. He was thirteen years old.

"Mom, my knee still hurts and it's really swollen!"

"Okay, let me take a look at it." To be honest, I really didn't think I was going to see anything, but just to appease him – after all, Cross Country had been finished for a month now…

What I saw completely shocked me! His left knee was swollen three times its normal size! It was so enlarged there were stretch marks on it! This wasn't the complaint of a thirteen-year-old boy who was trying to avoid something – this was something else all together!

Thus begun nine months of tests, doctor's visits and lastly, the suggestion of surgery to confirm the problem. After a few time-consuming misdiagnoses, and finally, knee surgery in May of 1997, at fourteen years old, Conner was identified with Rheumatoid Arthritis – specifically, Ankylosing Spondylitis. *Rheumatoid Arthritis is an immune system disorder. Rheumatoid arthritis is a chronic disorder for which there is no known cure.*[11]

Ankylosing spondylitis is a form of chronic inflammation of the spine and the sacroiliac joints. Ankylosing spondylitis is a systemic rheumatic disease, meaning it can affect other tissues throughout the body. Accordingly, it can cause inflammation in or injury to other joints away from the spine, as well as other organs, such as the eyes, heart, lungs, and kidneys.[12]

---

[11] The John Hopkins Arthritis Center
[12] MedicineNet.com

It was a tough diagnosis for a young boy. Fortunately, Conner was never interested in sports of any kind (I believe it was nature's way), and so it was easy enough for him to continue reading, drawing, and playing video games instead. If he wasn't able to kick a soccer ball around the field because his knees couldn't handle it – he was fine with that.

The worst symptom he had was the swelling, which was beginning to cause relentless pain. The surgery that May day removed the *synovium** from his left knee temporarily, curing most of the soreness he had.

I remember going into the recovery room to see him after the surgery. He was pretty out-of-it, of course. They had him on morphine drip, which they continued to give him by way of a PCA (Patient Controlled Anesthesia) pump during his three-day stay in the hospital. This was my son's first introduction to heroin.

"Morphine" as it is commonly referred to, is morphine sulfate. Heroin is diacetyl morphine. That is, heroin is simply morphine with an acetyl molecule attached.

In terms of effects, they are exactly the same -- and medically interchangeable -- except for dosage. In fact, they are both converted to the same form of morphine when they get into the body.

The only significant difference between them is that the acetyl molecule allows heroin to cross the blood-brain barrier more quickly than ordinary morphine. The result is that, in terms of dosage, heroin is about three times stronger. That is, one grain of heroin equals about three grains of morphine. Otherwise, they are identical.[13]

Now, that's not to say that his being on morphine caused his heroin addiction, of course.

There are thousands of people every day who have the need to use morphine post-operatively. But, interestingly, for certain people (usually having to do with genetics) when the dopamine receptors are opened in particular ways, one person is more likely to become an addict than others.

Along with everything else, Conner could very well have been one of those people.

---

[13] The Schaffer Library of Drug Policy, What is the difference between heroin and ordinary medical morphine?
*Synovium - thin membrane in freely moving joints that lines the joint capsule and secretes synovial fluid

TWENTY-EIGHT

The arthritis hadn't seemed to have traveled to any other part of his body, which was a very positive thing. The doctors were optimistic that Conner might live a fairly normal life (except for his ability to do any strenuous activity that might put too much pressure on his knees). They suggested that he would need a knee replacement eventually, but waiting until he was in his 40's or 50's if possible was best since knee replacement usually needs to be done every 20 years or so…

They also placed him on a medication called Methotrexate. *Methotrexate is an antimetabolite*. It interferes with the way cells utilize essential nutrients. As a result, Methotrexate inhibits the activity of the immune system, consequently reducing inflammation. As a cytotoxic**drug it may slow the rapid growth of cells in the synovial membrane that lines the joints.* [14]

When a patient is using Methotrexate they cannot drink alcohol. Methotrexate and alcohol can interact and damage your liver. Just as Conner was coming to the age where alcohol might be of interest, he was told he needed to avoid it.

---

[14] Carol & Richard Eustice, Methotrexate For Rheumatoid Arthritis
*Antimetabolite - a substance that interferes with growth of an organism by competing with or substituting for an essential nutrient in an enzymatic process.
**Cytotoxic drug - a substance that has a toxic effect on certain cells.

To be honest, I was relieved! Sam had always been a "partier." I never was. I didn't want my children to grow up thinking that they had to be high to have fun. Although Sam would never have admitted to it – his actions were quite clear – when you went out, you got high (one way or another), and the example it set didn't sit well with me.

To be fair to Sam, he was good about hiding it most of the time when the children were small. But I can still remember my youngest, Kim, at four years old asking me if "Daddy was at the baaa" (she didn't say her "R's" very well at that age), when her father was out in the evening.

It was obvious they noticed some of the things he did. I didn't want my children to have a sense that drinking or getting high was important to experience satisfaction. I had always tried to instill a belief in my children that life was worthwhile, all encompassing, and trustworthy. I hoped they would learn to enjoy the simple things, and appreciate the fundamental certainties that were within themselves.

At that point in my life I was going through enormous spiritual changes that would positively alter my viewpoint of myself (and life) forever. In my newfound strength I tried to guide Conner into a place where he would begin to relate to his own spiritual self.

I had plenty of opportunity to do this since Conner needed to go to physical therapy three days a week for the next six weeks. Each time we went, we went to lunch afterwards. We tried different restaurants – different kinds of foods. We talked, and laughed on many occasions. We played "slide" while waiting for his Orthopedic Surgeon, Dr. Yosh, to find the time for his follow-up exams. We discussed things while killing time at the Children's Hospital to have blood work done monthly. We shared ideas at Conner's rheumatologist's office every three months. And while I worked with him at home doing his physical therapy exercises, we laughed as we worked through the pain.

I not only grew closer to Conner on a spiritual level, our level of trust in one another was also cultivated. It was that trust that eventually led him to telling me his truth after he was released from Bay Run on the first day of May in 2007.

TWENTY-NINE

I was nervous going over to the North Side to pick Conner up. What was he going to look like? How was his attitude? Was he going to be okay? I just didn't know what to think…

As I drove up to the building I saw him standing there. His suitcases in hand, he looked anxious to get into the car. He opened the back door, threw his belongings onto the back seat, and climbed into the seat beside me.

He looked wonderful!

He looked fit, and clean.

His hair had been cut neatly, and he looked to be the picture of good health.

"Hi, Mom!" He smiled at me. His eyes were bright, and clear.

I leaned over and hugged him close to me. I didn't want to let him go. He chuckled quietly.

"It's okay, Mom. I'm okay. I'm GREAT, in fact!"

I pulled away from him, looked him in the eyes, and saw it. He WAS okay.

He was okay… (I thought it was all "over")

We began to drive home chitchatting about his ride from Wallingburg, Rhode Island. I kept looking over at him. He looked wonderful! It was like my son had come back to me. I forgot all my doubts and fears by the time we were home.

We spent the afternoon talking about some of the things he might need, and looking to see where and when the *Narcotics Anonymous*[15] meetings were held in our area. Conner explained that he needed to go to 90 meetings in 90 days. I also knew that he was supposed to go to Outpatient Care on the North Side for a while too. I asked him about that, but he said he'd call tomorrow. He just wanted to "be" at home today.

The purpose of adult intensive outpatient program is to provide a structured informational, educational and supportive therapeutic setting to identify significant clinical problems, which could interfere with the client's recovery from chemical dependency.

Treatment is individualized and may include individual, group and family sessions. The Intensive Outpatient Program can consist of up to 9 hours a week. [16]

---

[15] *Narcotics Anonymous is an international, community-based association of recovering drug addicts with more than 43,900 weekly meetings in over 127 countries worldwide.*, http://www.na.org/

[16] White Deer Run, Adult Services

Little did I know that "tomorrow" would never come.

THIRTY

We spent the rest of the day eating Arby's for lunch, and shopping for a new XBOX, and games. He convinced me that he needed it so he wouldn't be tempted to relapse. I had done a lot of research, and I understood the disease a lot better now. I understood that it truly was a disease. I understood the many characteristics that point to addiction. I understood the risk factors. I even understood that manipulation, lying, and stealing were "normal" behaviors for an addict – a side effect of the need for a fix.

Nevertheless, he was able to employ my sympathies and concerns. I spent $450.00 on a brand new XBOX, and several games so he'd stay sober. (I can fix it!)

That night he went to his first meeting. I thought everything was fine.

THIRTY-ONE

Sam and I never really "dated." He started coming over to my house just a couple of weeks after school started in August of 1971. I don't even know how he knew where I lived.

I was just coming out of a relationship, and didn't see him as "the man I would marry." Actually, I didn't see him as a "man" at all.

He stood less than five feet tall at the time, very skinny, sported a curly blond Afro, and never came over clear-headed. He had been drinking, smoking weed or had been doing something else each time he arrived. It was difficult to take him seriously. He was funny, though.

Each time he came over, it was a short visit. He rarely came inside the house. And he always made me laugh.

Perhaps what he did more than anything was give me attention. And it was that kind of interest that I sorely needed.

I know now (because he told me) that the only reason he was coming over to my house, and giving me attention at all was because he thought I was "easy." I had mentioned to a friend in Math class that my "boyfriend" and I were wrestling, and Sam (having overheard what I said) took it as a sexual connotation. He figured I'd be an easy lay!

He was very wrong!

I had never been with a man (or a boy). I had only just learned to "French" kiss. In fact, I was so naïve, that I had only just learned how people made babies! For a sixteen-year-old girl, I was very innocent (even by early 1970's standards).

It was obvious that he wanted more than a chummy relationship, but I can honestly say that I was not in any way attracted to him that way. In fact, I rather felt sorry for him. Although he had a great sense of humor, he seemed lonely somewhere deep inside. He appeared to be very self-assured, but I noticed that the way he seemed to feel most powerful was when he was bullying someone or playing class clown. He was rude to the teaching staff at school, and always pushing the limits of what he could get away with. To me, that pointed to insecurity. (And if there was anything I could easily relate to, it was insecurity)!

I'm sure that's why my "fix it" mind-set started with him.

Maybe I could make him happy.

Maybe he could fulfill something in my heart – that empty space where I felt so unnecessary.

Of course, these were all psychological responses that I was completely unaware of at the time.

I believed I might make a positive difference in his life.

I felt good about that.

THIRTY-TWO

There is no question that people who regularly attend support group meetings and "work the program" are more likely to recover and less likely to relapse. Many people are able to recover through participation in 12-step and other mutual help groups alone. Participating in support groups is not necessary for recovery to occur, but it helps. One advantage of support groups is that they are free, widely available and focused on recovery.[17]

Conner attended a meeting on Wednesday, Thursday, Friday, and Saturday. He came home enthusiastically about a couple of them – even mentioning that someone he went to school with was a member of one. He was taking showers every day, keeping his room much cleaner than he had in the past, and he was home with us (except when he was at an N.A. meeting), and he seemed upbeat, confident, and healthy.

In fact, he was probably overconfident. He kept putting off calling Bay Run for his aftercare saying that he didn't really think he needed it. He was fine! He felt GREAT! It was difficult to argue with him. He did seem fine…

Sunday evening he went to a meeting. He left happy, and positive like he had been doing since

---

[17] Mark Willenbring, M.D., HBO Addiction, Recovery: An Addicted Person's Responsibilities

arriving home. His father and I were comfortable and hopeful.

That night he never came home.

THIRTY-THREE

The winter that Conner turned 14 years old – just four days before his birthday, he was awarded the Eagle Scout award. *The fact that a boy is an Eagle Scout has always carried with it a special significance, not only in Scouting but also as he enters higher education, business or industry, and community service. The award is a performance-based achievement whose standards have been well maintained over the years. Not every boy who joins a Boy Scout troop earns the Eagle Scout rank; only about 5 percent of all Boy Scouts do so.*[18]

Within a week of receiving his Eagle Scout award Conner was also voted into the Order of the Arrow, which is Scouting's National Honor Society. *OA is recognized as the BSA's national brotherhood of honor campers.*[19]

Both of these honors were well deserved. Admittedly, I helped Conner quite a bit with some of the planning of his Eagle project – however, it was a much larger endeavor than most boys attempt. Still, although I helped him, he is the one who completed all the other requirements on his own, and with the work he did during the project itself – the leadership he commanded in such a mature way – he was more than deserving of his award.

---

[18] Boy Scouts of America, Eagle Scouts
[19] Boy Scouts of America, Order of the Arrow, OA Basics

He was the youngest Boy Scout in Troop 19 to ever have achieved this award.

His recognition into the Order of the Arrow only a few days later was an incredible pat on the back from his fellow campers and troop leaders.

We were so proud of him that day. His father smiled at him as his award was pinned on. A tear filled my eye. He was still a little boy, but that day he stood as tall as a man!

THIRTY-FOUR

We had waited all night Sunday for Conner to come home. I was unable to sleep because I was filled with worry! When I finally got in touch with Conner at Madison's house on Monday morning he told me that everything was fine.

"I just wanted to see how Madison was doing, Mom, and ended up spending the night." He explained how he'd gone to the meeting in Pembrooke (which I later found out was not true), and then drove over to Madison's (since it was so close anyway) for a visit.

While he was away at Bay Run there was a stringent suggestion that he stay away from people and places that might trigger a relapse. Among other things, *addicted people must learn how to avoid contact with the triggers that may set in motion their brain's demanding cry for drugs.*[20]

"Conner, I don't think you should be over there. You know you're supposed to avoid any triggers."

(Okay, so now that he knows what I think – he'll listen to Mommy, and do just what he is supposed to do)

"Mom, I'm fine. I'm not going to use. I'm just visiting for a while. I'll be home later."

---

[20] HBO Addiction, Avoiding Relapse, Aftercare

"Conner, did you do anything? Tell me…" I begged. I couldn't believe that Conner was where he was without doing some kind of drug! Madison's house was filled with nothing but addicts – at least three of them were using heroin (including Madison). How could he possibly have been there for over twelve hours and not gotten high?

I knew the facts. According to Dr. Anna Rose Childress, *"The motivation to seek a drug, once triggered, can feel overwhelming and sometimes leads to very poor decision-making: the user will pursue the drug, despite potentially disastrous future negative consequences (and many past negative consequences)".* [21]

He paused, "I did smoke a little weed, but it's fine. I'm not going use heroin, Mom. I'm done with that! I'm fine."

I argued with him that it's not okay to do weed. He has to stay completely sober. It's too soon to think that anything is safe. In fact, using anything is never going to be okay. He has to avoid all of it. He has to avoid those people!

(Okay – now he knows what to do….)

---

[21] Anna Rose Childress, Ph.D., HBO Addiction, What is Relapse?

"I'll be home this afternoon, Mom. Don't worry. I'm fine."

Conner hadn't really changed that much.

He had experienced some depression and behavioral therapy, he was detoxed, he was learning some things about accountability – but it had only been three weeks. Recovery is a lifetime journey. The first ninety days are critical. *The first year, as well as the second, are decisive milestones. The most dangerous period for lapse is the first 3-6 months after completion of formal treatment. Relapse, defined as return to excessive or problematic use, is less common, occurring in approximately 20-30% of those who complete formal care in the prior year.*[22]

When I came home from work that evening Conner was there. He did seem fine. He didn't look high.

But for me, the fear was returning – the uncertainty was palpable. Sam's attitude told me that he was very doubtful.

We ate dinner, and I left to go my second job hoping Conner would be home when I got back – but knowing he might not…

---

[22] A. Thomas McLellan, M.D., HBO Addiction, Treatment is Over, Now What If a Relapse Happens?

THIRTY-FIVE

Over the course of the next few days Conner went to one or two meetings (or so he said), and began hanging out with Madison every day. I couldn't shake the concern I had even through his adamant argument that he was "fine."

While Conner was away at Bay Run I had gotten his car detailed, and replaced the flat tire. The broken window was fixed, and the inside as well as the outside of the car was immaculate!

It was my gift to him for the hard work he'd put in and the wonderful accomplishment of getting clean. It was supposed to be the symbol of a new beginning.

By the end of that first week home, Conner's mirror was broken again, and there appeared to be a new scratch on the car…

"Conner, what are you doing? Why is your mirror off again?" (It was a common theme when he was using heroin to see his mirror hanging off the side of his car. It's what a drug dealer does if you rip him off – a kind of "first warning.")

"I don't know how that happened!" He was angry. That kind of anger was another sign that he had begun abusing drugs again.

"Conner, are you getting high? Please just tell me what's going on…" I needed to know.

"I've smoked weed a couple times, okay – had a few drinks. I'm fine! I don't have to put up with this!" And he left.

Now I was really upset! Where was he going? What was he going to do?

But I knew where he was going, and I knew what he was going to do. I wasn't fooling myself. Still, I wanted to hide it from Sam. Maybe Sam would think everything was okay – that Conner was okay – and he wouldn't reject him again…

Although I was "protecting" my son – I was actually enabling him once more.

In a relationship where one individual has an addiction, a loved one often becomes over-involved in the addict's life. They frequently demonstrate enabling behaviors such as trying to "fix the addict" or to "rescue them." Very often the codependent person feels deeply responsible for the addicted person. All they talk and think about is the problem their loved one is facing. They often also feel it is their job to stop the addict from his addiction.

The partner that is "enabling" is not responsible for their loved one's addictions. However, when the partner cleans up after, or covers for the addict, they are enabling the addict not to face the consequences of their actions. The codependent becomes more upset about the problem than the person who has the addiction. It is very hard for an enabler to let the consequences fall on the addict, because usually they are very fearful. Codependents can feel terrified of losing the addict. They know that if their loved one gets in trouble at work they may lose their job. Often codependents grew up with parents who had addictions or other emotional issues. Codependence and enabling are often learned behaviors.[23]

And if I was anything most of my life it was codependent!

---

[23] Essortment, What is co-dependence?

THIRTY-SIX

I felt an intense need to be needed – to be important – to be loved.

My mother had verbally, emotionally, and physically abused me. My sister had betrayed me. My home was not a safe haven. My ability to trust was really only a hope that I might be able to trust something someday. It was not based in fact. The facts were: I had nowhere to turn, and no one to turn to.

My stepfather (known as "Big Bob" to everyone in the neighborhood) was a big man. He stood 6 foot 4 inches tall, and his waistline was about 55 inches. He sported a grey beard, a full head of beautifully matching hair, and brown eyes. He was like a big teddy bear – mostly gentle and quiet. Rarely did we see his temper. I actually think my stepfather was afraid to lose control – I think he was fearful that if he lost control he just might really hurt someone.

You see, at 18 years of age my stepfather was out with three other friends, and they decided to rob a neighborhood grocery store. I don't really know the details, but somehow or other, the owner of the store was shot dead. All four boys were arrested, and put in jail. The shooter was given a life sentence. My stepfather and his other two friends were given 25 years.

While my stepfather was in jail he studied animal husbandry. *Animal husbandry is the science of taking care of domestic animals that are used primarily as food or product sources. Anyone who takes care of domesticated animals, especially in large groups, is practicing animal husbandry.*[24] He always loved animals, and hoped to become a forest ranger after being released from Northern Penitentiary. Unfortunately, you can't be a forest ranger when you've been found guilty of murder…

He was released after 18 years – just four years before he married my mother.

My stepfather and I had a pretty comfortable relationship. We would walk down into the woods on Sunday mornings – sometimes staying until late afternoon. My stepfather was the person who taught me to love and appreciate nature. We'd look for salamanders under rocks or sit somewhere quietly awaiting the arrival of any woodland creatures that might venture close to us.

He talked to me about nature – taught me about the leaves, and the trees. He showed me the beauty of a summer thunderstorm. He always said that nature was his church. I felt very close to him.

My mother and stepfather married when my sister and I were four years old. He was a cousin

---

[24] Wise Geek, What is Animal Husbandry?

of the husband of her best friend. They met, dated, and were married within six months.

It was a marriage of convenience. My mother wanted out of the housing project. My stepfather wanted out of his mother's house.

I don't know if my parents ever had sexual relations. I tend to doubt that they did from what each of them told me over the years. But it was a consistent existence. My mother ran the show. My stepfather brought in the money (what little there was of it).

When I was about fourteen or fifteen years old my stepfather began saying things to me that were sexual in content. I didn't really know what to think about that. I remember "feeling" that it wasn't right, but I didn't "know" it wasn't right.

It was abnormal in the 1960's to discuss these kinds of things anyway, but for him to make comments like, "I'd like to really show you what it would be like" (referring to having sex) simply was over the top (even by today's much looser standards).

He'd mention all manner of sexual things to me, and I never quite knew how to respond. So.... I laughed – even commented back to him on some level. To be honest, I didn't really know what sex was – not really. I was inexperienced, and very green around the edges. If I was egging him on, I wasn't even aware of it.

I remember one day he opened the bathroom door as I was dressing. I spun around quickly so he wouldn't see my newly developing breasts. He asked what it was that I was hiding.

"Nothing…" I replied, "I'm getting dressed."

"You don't have to be embarrassed. They're perfectly natural – no big deal." (What was it that he was trying to convince me of?)

"I'm not embarrassed." (Yes, I am – please close the door!)

"I'm just saying, if I saw your tits there wouldn't be anything wrong with that. Besides, they're not even that big – you only have little mosquito bites there…" He seemed to be trembling. I didn't understand. What did he want me to do – show them to him?

"I know there's nothing wrong. It's just weird."

"It's not that weird," he said.

My mind was racing! I was not any good at confrontation at all. Any time I had tried to stand up for myself I had gotten a beating, and then had to deal with the painful welts that reminded me to keep quiet.

He was my stepfather – does that make it okay? I didn't know. I just knew that I wanted him to leave.

In a confused rage I turned around, breasts exposed, and said to him, "There! Okay?"

And then I turned around again mortified, but not sure why.

THRITY-SEVEN

I had worked all day the following Saturday. Conner had been home from Bay Run for eleven days.

When I walked in the door Sam was really upset.

These days Sam getting upset doesn't affect me the way it used to. For most of my married life I tried to appease his anger, make peace somehow, and try to "fix it." If I could make him happy, then he'd be happy. His anger frightened me most of those early years.

After a good amount of therapy I realized that I wasn't actually fearful of my husband – it was my mother that I was frightened of.

Sam screamed, belittled, name-called, blamed, and became irrational. He was a narcissist, and Conner and I shared the honor of being his victims most of the time. But Sam didn't hit. He didn't burn me. He didn't spit in my face. So, for some reason, just yelling or threatening me didn't seem as awful.

Still, I could tell that whatever it was that was bothering him, it was really bad.

"What's wrong?" My mind was speeding. Fear was caught in my throat.

"He fucking stole my weed!" Sam screamed. "I thought it was okay. I thought it was safe, so I let my guard down, and that asshole stole my weed!"

"Are you sure?" (I could only hope Sam was wrong) "Maybe you put it somewhere else…"

He glared at me (the way my mother used to when she was enraged). He screamed, "YES, I'M SURE! Do you think I'm stupid? I know where I left it! I didn't put it somewhere else! Stop trying to defend him! He's a liar! He's getting high again, and he's using MY stuff to do it!"

"When he comes in, we'll ask him…" I thought if I were reasonable, Sam would be too.

"I don't need to ask him! I just need to kill him! I'm sick of this shit! I'm sick of my stuff being stolen! I'm sick of his ass-hole-ness! Why does he treat me like a dog?!?!"

Just then I saw Conner coming up the walk.

I ran to the door with a look of warning on my face, "Sit down, Conner."

He looked innocent. "What's wrong?" I hadn't told his father that he was drinking and smoking weed again. We had never actually told him that Conner was using heroin. Sam was told that Conner felt he had a drug problem (I guess everything but heroin, and that's why he'd gone to rehab).

Sam's face was red. He had an ugly expression on his face that represented frustration, rage, disappointment, and fear.

I looked at Conner. "Daddy's missing some weed. Did you take it?"

Conner got quiet. He knew there was no way to deny it. "Yes. I'm sorry…"

"WHY? WHY?" Sam screamed. "What the Hell is wrong with you? Are you a complete Asswipe? Can't you do anything right? Jesus Christ, Conner. Why did you go to rehab if you're just going to come out, and start doing that shit again?

"That is MY stuff! MINE! Not yours! MINE!"

I needed Sam to calm down. I knew that he could get violent – I'd seen it before – and I didn't want it to get to that point. I just wanted to help Conner.

"Honey, what's going on? Why would you do take Daddy's stuff?"

Conner closed his eyes. A tear spilled down each cheek. "I don't know. I don't know. I'm nothing but a fuck up."

"You got THAT right! It's all you've ever been!" his father piped in.

Conner bent over – his face in his hands, and began to cry.

"Help us understand, Sweetie."

"I ALREADY understand! He's an asshole! He doesn't care about anyone but himself.
He certainly doesn't care about me or he wouldn't do something like this! How you can steal from your own family? What's wrong with you?"

"Dad," Conner said with tears swelling in his eyes – his nose running – "I went into rehab because I was using heroin – not just a few drugs. Now that I'm out, I'm trying to avoid doing heroin – so I just smoke weed a little."

"MY WEED! MINE – NOT YOURS!" (Why was it always about him)?

"I know. I'm sorry. I don't blame you for hating me. I hate myself."

"I know what you've been doing! Do you think I'm stupid? I've known since we found that needle in the summer!"

I looked over at Sam with pleading eyes. I was asking him to stop screaming. I was asking him to reach out.

There have been very few times in my life when I've seen Sam find any kind of compassion, understanding, empathy or kindness. I know that sounds incredibly shocking but it is true – especially when it came to Conner.

This became one of those times.

In the blink of an instant Sam's tone quieted (a little). He said, "You've got to beat this, Conner. You can't keep doing this shit." He was very firm – in control – but he wasn't screaming any more.

"I know...."

"No, I mean it. I know people that use this kind of shit. It'll ruin your life. You've got to stop!"

"Only one out of twenty people make it." Conner replied (pulling from what he'd learned in recovery).

"Well, you're going to be that one out of twenty. You have to be." Sam said.

It was a strange kind of encouragement. Conner rarely heard anything from his father that sounded like support (if ever, really).

"You just have to." Sam said. And then he went upstairs.

I went over to my son, and hugged him. He cried.

"Did you hear him, Conner? He believes in you. He wants you to succeed!"

"I know." Conner whimpered, "That's why I'm crying."

Sam came back downstairs. I looked at him. He knew what I wanted. He found the strength, and he hugged Conner.

It was a moment that was healing for all of us. It wasn't the end of the crisis, but it was a small beginning in the recovery of Conner's heart.

THIRTY-EIGHT

Like hypertension or diabetes, addiction is a lifelong illness.

Biological and behavioral factors influence addiction, as they do other chronic conditions.

Addiction can be effectively treated and managed through lifestyle changes and, in some cases, the use of medication.

For hundreds of years, people have considered addiction to be a problem of willpower or of moral failing. Now we know that addiction is a disorder much like other chronic illnesses that involve behavior and lifestyle. Some of these illnesses begin with voluntary behaviors, such as poor nutrition or failure to exercise. But then, biological changes occur in the body to make the illness a chronic condition.

Most people who have chronic conditions, even those who are working hard to stay on top of their illness, sometimes eat poorly or do other things that they know aren't healthy. They backslide, or relapse, at some point.

Other diseases like this include:
- *Hypertension (high blood pressure)*
- *Adult onset (type 2) diabetes*
- *Atherosclerosis (hardening of the arteries)*

These diseases are similar because they are:

- *Chronic*
- *Influenced by biological and behavioral factors*
- *Incurable, but can be effectively treated and managed*[25]

---

[25] HBO Addiction, A Chronic Condition

THIRTY-NINE

The next day we drove to Clarksville. We have a house in Ripley Township on fifty-seven acres of mostly wild land. It's a haven away from the city, and a quiet resting place for the soul. It was just what we needed.

Sam spent the weekend working all around the property as usual. Conner read a book. I wrote in my journal, read a little, and played solitaire.

We ate leisurely, and enjoyed television in the evening.

Nothing else was said about the weed.

I felt that we might have turned a corner. I felt encouraged. I have always known that if there were one thing missing in Conner's life that he desperately needed, it was the encouragement and acceptance of his father. I began to believe that after Sam reached out to Conner they might both be feeling warmer toward one another and that the love Conner felt might promote healing for him on many levels.

Instead, it was the calm before the storm!

FORTY

A few days later I came home from work in the evening to find the dog in his crate, and neither Conner nor Sam home.

I changed my clothes, and went on-line to check my e-mail.

I was only home about twenty minutes when Sam came in red-faced, and a bit drunk.

He started to tell me that his nephew, John, had seen Conner with Madison at the Dairy Mart, and that they both seemed really "high."

I didn't know what to say. The feeling that moved through my body was a mixture of fear and exhaustion. I didn't know if I could do this again…

I was completely addicted to my son's addiction at this point.

Sam started to tell me that he had been out with his buddies, and that they spent a good amount of time talking about Conner, and what Conner has done to Sam – what he's made him "go through" – how Sam's "suffered."

Then, as proudly as anyone could, he told me that his friends had offered to beat Conner up to "knock some sense into him!"

"My friends really care about me, and they'll do whatever they can do for me so I don't have to go through any more shit. If I have to do more than beat him up to stop this bullshit, then I'll do something more! I know people. You don't realize the kind of people I know."

(Was he informing me or warning me?)

"What are you saying?" I asked. "They're going to beat him up? (You're going to beat up your own son?) What's that going to do? Sam, this is a disease. Don't you think he feels awful about everything?"

"No, I don't think he feels awful. I don't think he cares. And if he's going to do these things, he's not my son." (WHAT?) "I'll do whatever I have to, to make him stop. I'm tired of him stealing my shit!"

(Who are you? Whom did I marry?)

I remember feeling frightened, and as if I was backed into some kind of nightmarish corner. How could I stop Sam's friends from harming our child? He was an adult child but he was still our flesh and blood. His disease had turned him into someone neither of us recognized on many levels, but he was still Conner. Underneath the stigma of addiction - he was still Conner.

There was suddenly a pressing need to make sure Conner was okay. I felt an overwhelming need to rescue my son from his father as well as from the addiction that was slowly claiming his life. I was like a mother bear that would take a bullet rather than risk her own cub's existence,

I realized, after the shock of what Sam was proposing wore off, that because of Sam's inability to express any real emotion except anger, he was actually considering having Conner beat up because he cared about him. Although some of Sam's concern certainly was focused on his own well-being, and that of his "stuff," in some twisted, unacceptable way, Sam was so scared he felt like he had no other options, and was unable to think of any other way to handle the situation.

This didn't make it okay. It only helped me not to hate my husband in that moment.

It's an interesting reality that most people are under the impression that someone who is addicted to something - whether it is drugs, alcohol, food, gambling or whatever - doesn't want to stop. It's certainly possible, depending on the addiction, and the personality of the person involved, that they are unaware of their own inability, and believe they are in control. But when the time comes to stop - they simply can't.

One thing that really struck me about the night my husband told me he was planning on beating Conner up to "knock some sense into him" was that he actually believed it would work! He thought that Conner was just being foolish.

It may have been an irresponsible choice to begin with, and it may have been irrational at some point, but at this point Conner's brain had gone through physical changes - his frontal cortex was damaged - and the addiction was in control. It was as if he had been possessed by an evil demon.

And, in fact, he was...

FORTY-ONE

"It is in our nature to gravitate to what we believe is safe and familiar – even if our version of safe is a mirage."

-Jeffery A. Brown

Throughout our relationship Sam had experienced many temper tantrums. I remember a few of them specifically. I remember being afraid. Then again, I was used to being afraid. I had never lived day-to-day without it...

Still, I wasn't afraid with him the way I had been with my mother. Throughout most of our marriage, the fear was that he'd leave me, and I'd be alone again. I had never been given the emotional support in my life that allowed me to yet know the extent of my own worth or strength.

Ours had always been a strange relationship – free from normal commitment. For instance, when Sam and I were dating I didn't fuss when he decided to date another girl for about a year while he was still seeing me too. I didn't let him know how I felt when he promised to come over, and ended up going out with his friends to drink again (this happened quite frequently). I didn't get jealous. I didn't start arguments. I had sex with him whenever he wanted it. I was completely subservient to him. I took responsibility for everything that ever went wrong.

Looking back – I'm aware that he didn't really treat me with respect. Still, for me, it was so much better than what I was used to. Since I had never been given any kind of respect, I don't suppose I even knew what it was, to be honest. And besides, I could make him happy. I had a purpose in my heart. I loved him.

Sam and I spent 9 ½ years together before we actually got married. Our marriage was rather matter-of-fact. We were making a trip to Kentucky to move his uncle, and figured we might as well do it while there.

Our families were not in attendance. Instead we had a Justine of the Peace, and two Probation officers for witnesses. The whole thing cost us $35.00!

When we got home from Kentucky we went to our separate houses, and finally moved into a newly acquired apartment on the fourth day of our marriage.

At this writing I've known Sam for 38 years, and I don't know if Sam and I have really ever had a heart to heart discussion. He's not a deep thinker, and has always felt that I was too much of one. If a conversation starts, and he's not interested, he lets you know by interrupting what you're saying with something he wants to say or he just completely ignores you all together.

If a discussion starts that actually needs his attention, he always turns it into an issue that will end with his screaming and blaming. He doesn't like me much, although I do believe he loves me as much as he is capable of loving anyone.

Sam's insecurities have caused him to become a batterer. I wouldn't have known that before August of 2001. I always thought that if someone were a batterer they were the kind of person that hit another person. I thought battery was physical.

There are characteristics that indicate someone is a batterer. Some of them include:

- *They try to control victims.*

- *They have Jekyll and Hyde personalities.*

- *Jealousy*

- *They have explosive tempers -- they fly into rages without provocation.*

- *They tell victims it is all their fault - they project their own faults onto victims.*

- *They use verbal assault in addition to physical assault (insults, put downs, slanderous names).*

- *They come from families where violence*

was practiced.[26]

These characteristics are typical of Sam's behavior. Certainly some days are worse than others. His moods seem to come in waves (another trait of battering conduct). And the jealousy he seems to feel comes – not from other men – but from my children – particularly Conner.

The way I learned to "cope" with Sam's anger was a slow trial-and-error process of attempting to open up our lines of communication.

Over the years I tried just about everything. There were times when he frightened me so much all I could do was cry and beg his forgiveness. Other times I would simply agree with him. Sometimes I would get very, very quiet, and for a very short time I even tried screaming back at him. I tried getting him to talk it out. I walked out of the room a few times, and other times I tried to hug him. I even tried sex…

I avoided some of his screaming by holding back information from him. If he didn't know, he wouldn't scream, and somehow or other that helped me not have to deal with the terror I would feel.

Incredibly, these reactions – these trial-and-error methods became second nature to me after a

---

[26] Laura Wetzel, Counselor at A Woman's Place, City of Olivette Police Department

while. In fact, to this day – even knowing that none of them would work – I have a tendency to take the easier route when feasible. Since conversation isn't a possibility, I just evade issues that are going to require it. I take care of everything myself, and if it's something he must know – although I eventually tell him – I wait as long as possible.

There were times, early in my therapy, when my counselor used to ask me why I chose to act that way. She'd say, "If he's going to scream at you one way or the other, why not just get it over with?" Later on we came to the conclusion that it wasn't necessarily a conscious choice, but a conditioned response.

I have begun to ask myself, "How long does it take to erase fifty years of fear reactions?" I have come to the conclusion that the more aware I am that I'm doing it, the more it becomes a choice. When I'm aware of the choice, it's not about conditioning – it's about avoidance.

There are obviously many things I need to continue to work on.

I have a lot of personal strength. In fact, I am one of the strongest women I know. I'm sure most of it is innate or I wouldn't have come out of my circumstances so optimistically. I am a philosophical and spiritual person. Although I'm not perfect in any sense of the word, I believe in myself. I have an almost inhuman ability for compassion, and the patience of a saint.

What I have learned in all my years with Sam is that the only person I should be is me.

To be fair to Sam – he's certainly not all bad. I can't say as I've ever met a more honest person. His work ethic is excellent. He's extremely talented. He has a wonderful sense of humor. He has a sense of detachment that is amazing. He loves nature. People who know him really like and respect him. He's intelligent – and intuitive (in many, but not all ways).

I married a fundamentally good man.

But he is a good man who doesn't really know "how" to allow himself the freedom to love fully. He feels vulnerable if he lets down his guard. He's unaware of his own trust issues. He's not self-examining, and so he doesn't see that the things he says and does are hurtful sometimes. He takes no responsibly for anything that he thinks is going wrong. He is always right.

His insecurities have bathed him in fear. And his fear makes him lose his temper no matter what the circumstances are. He doesn't express joy or worry.

He expresses anger.

This was so for my mother. It is so for my husband.

What I have always needed to know was that there wasn't anything wrong with me. It's what Conner needed to know too.

FORTY-TWO

For two decades, researchers have been struggling to identify the biological and environmental risk factors that can lead to addiction to alcohol and other drugs. These factors form a complex mélange in which the influences combine to bring about addiction and to make its treatment challenging.

"The people most likely to get addicted are the ones who also have other problems," says Dr. Mark Willenbring, who directs the Division of Treatment and Recovery Research of the National Institute on Alcohol Abuse and Alcoholism (NIAAA).[27]

Many, if not most, people who are addicted to alcohol or other drugs suffer from another mental health disorder at some point.

People with addiction and co-occurring mental and medical health disorders must be treated for both kinds of disorders at the same time to improve the likelihood of recovery.[28]

Conner was diagnosed with ADD when he was 19 years old – a bit late in life for that kind of conclusion, but it answered a lot of long standing questions we'd had concerning some of his behavioral quirks.

---

[27] HBO Addiction, Why Do Some People Become Addicted
[28] HBO Addiction, Co-occurring Disorders

Along with ADD, and Ankylosing Spondylitis, Conner's self-esteem was in the toilet, he didn't trust his world, he didn't feel lovable, had no emotional tools to deal with personal adversity, and he was chronically depressed. Add on top of these things an addiction to heroin; the challenges he faced were unimaginable!

This is probably why Conner relapsed.

He didn't admit to it right away, of course, but I knew. All the signs were there: he stopped coming home, another side mirror was broken on his car, and he was asking me for money again. His Xbox was gone. I'd still be paying on it for a couple more years, though I'd find out later that it had been sold for $125.00 – enough for one day's worth of heroin. Mike Petro was calling the house again.

I asked him.

He denied it.

I knew.

On Saturday, November 17th I came home from work to find Madison at my house with Conner. Sam didn't like Madison being there. Neither did I. Although I have since found out that it was Mike that introduced Conner to mainlining, we believed (and still do) that if Conner hadn't begun hanging around with Madison and her family of opiate addicts, he might never have tried heroin to begin with.

We never felt that she was good for Conner.

When Conner met Madison she was thirteen years old. He was twenty. Madison was born into a poor family who trusted in the Welfare system to pay their bills. Her mother was dying of cervical cancer. Her father had black lung, and was a heavy marijuana smoker. Both of her brothers, her sister, and her sister's boyfriend, Josh were heroin addicts.

Madison was the youngest. She had learned early on that one had to fight for what they wanted, and to control whomever they could to get it. She was a scheming, calculating person who (surprisingly) had a certain kind of innocence too. She was very young.

I believe her family was a loving family.

But Madison wanted out.

She didn't want to leave her parents; she wanted to leave her circumstances.

Conner fulfilled a need she had. He was a loving father figure. He spent money on her. He took her places.

But the more he did, the more she wanted. The more she expected.

Conner needed to feel necessary. He needed to feel loved; Madison's parents accepted and cared about him. He held down a job at that time, and had a car. They respected him - something Conner desperately needed. Madison made him feel important.

Their relationship was codependent.

They didn't lift one another up, but they did hold onto one another as they both sunk further down. Like life preservers filled with sand – when they were with one another they were both drowning.

So there they were – Madison sitting on Conner's bed, Conner lying down. The TV was on. Both of them were nodding off. They had that, "I just did heroin a little while ago" look to them.

I awoke Conner.

"What's going on, Conner?" I was angry.

"Whaaaa…. What do you mean?" His words stumbled out.

"Are you high?"

"No… I'm just sleepy…" He started to scratch himself.

Opiates[29] cause an allergic reaction that causes most people to feel itchy. Scratching and nodding are two tell tale signs of recent heroin use.

"Why are you so itchy, Conner?"

His eyes were drooping... Madison was still only half conscious sitting on the bed. I pushed his shoulder. His eyes shot open. "Huhhhhh...."

"Why are you so itchy?"

"I don't know... I took some pills of Josh's....*Oxycontin*...."[30]

"How many did you take?" I didn't believe him.

"I don't know. Seven or eight?"

"Seven or eight! Conner you could overdose on that amount!" Now I was a little afraid.

Madison woke up.

"Whaaat?" she stammered. "Conner why digew take those? You shon't do that, baby." She was slurring as badly as he was.

I walked out of the room.

---

[29] Any of various sedative narcotics containing opium or one or more of its natural or synthetic derivatives.
[30] Oxycontin (Oxycotin) is a narcotic pain reliever.

It was obvious that Madison wasn't going home tonight.

I unwound watching TV. Sam was pissed. I prayed he wouldn't start another fight. I just couldn't take it tonight! Finally we went to bed.

At four-thirty in the morning Conner woke me up. He was acting perfectly normal – not high, and certainly not sleepy.

"I'm going to ride Mike somewhere. I'll be right back. I'm fine, Mom."

What? Why is he waking me up about that? Looking at the clock I understood. It was almost morning. I guess he thought I'd get up and notice his car was missing…

The time had come to talk to him.

I jumped out of the bed, and went downstairs, but he was just pulling away.

Mike Petro was the final piece to the puzzle. Going to see Mike Petro meant that he was really going to get heroin.

FORTY-THREE

There are plenty of people who would have thought that at this point Conner should not have been allowed to live in our house any longer. They might wonder what I was thinking - WHY wouldn't I just kick him out! I don't know if there will ever be words to describe how it feels to see your child in this condition - with this kind of life-threatening problem.

Perhaps it would have been better for everyone had I told him to leave. It's what his father wanted to do. Maybe that's why I didn't want to. His father, (in my opinion), had caused a lot of Conner's insecurities. If Sam thought it was a good idea (whether he was right in that moment or not), I couldn't help but think it wasn't.

At some point Conner took Madison home. I don't really remember when. It was the Sunday before Easter. I asked him to come home after he delivered her or to (at least) call me.

I needed to talk to him. I knew that he was using. I knew that he needed to get back into rehab. I knew that he had no self-control.

(I needed to save him)!

FORTY-FOUR

By 1987 Sam and I had three children: Conner, Sydney and Kim. We owned our own home. Sam was trying to find work again. He had been laid off for various reasons (none of his own making) three times in the six years we'd been married. We had a car payment, and mounting bills from a growing family. Furnace, stove, and refrigerator replacements had to be charged. Shoes and school clothing had to be charged. The needs that surround five people are incredibly expensive when the person who is providing 95% of the income or more is only making minimum wage.

For a long time I didn't tell Sam how high the bills were getting because I didn't want him to feel bad. I protected him. I enabled him...

He fussed all the time about not being a good provider, and knowing how hard he tried – he worked very diligently – I couldn't bring myself to explain that our debt was getting unmanageable.

There was an egotistical issue on my part as well. Sam's mother was always so good about money. In fact, she was incredible! I wanted to be just like her (so Sam would respect me); if I admitted that I wasn't balancing the budget well enough, he'd be very disappointed with me. (Everything's always my fault, after all)

The bigger matter, though, was always that he felt so inadequate, and my empathy took over the logic that would normally have been necessary in that kind of situation.

Besides, I didn't feel comfortable attempting a conversation with him about this kind of thing. Aside from the awareness that he would be upset (and I was increasingly very frightened of his anger), our discussions were usually superficial. Having a heart-to-heart wasn't our forte'.

Unfortunately, this went on for years. He'd get a job, and lose it. For a while he started his own business, and working 18-hour days he was still only bringing home about $4.50 an hour. The kids were getting bigger, our needs were getting more expensive, and I was only working as a part-time childbirth educator, and baby-sitter.

More charges.

More debt.

I tried to consolidate. Then I had two bills – a big one and a little one.

I tried again. Then I had two big bills, and eventually a third.

Over and over again the mounting debt became overwhelming! I kept trying. I kept failing. It was my fault. I was doing something wrong.

I tried paying them off, and then something else would come up, and I'd end up with no money so I'd have to charge again. It was a vicious cycle I have yet to find myself free of.

Still, I couldn't tell him. When he finally got a pretty good job making $8.00 an hour, and eventually $10 or $12 an hour, and I was working a bit more – our income was greater – the bills were so horrendous that I became fearful rather than compassionate.
I was no longer worried about his ego. Anytime I tried to explain that we had debt he would start screaming at me, and blaming me for not doing what I was supposed to do. He called me names, and made me feel just awful. I was also worried about his being so angry that he'd leave me.

He'd threatened it before – many times: "I'll leave all of you. I don't care if I see the kids again. YOU can take care of them. I'll divorce you all!"

I was still unaware that I was strong enough to do whatever it took to care for my family. I was frightened of being without him. I wanted the kids to have a "real" family.

I continued to keep the bills to myself, and they continued to escalate!

I had lived my life thus far in a perpetual state of perilous fear and insecurity. I had never known what a healthy relationship could be, and was mutually dependent on every person to provide even the most basic human needs: love, safety, and acceptance.

These were the essential kinds of things I never knew first hand. I was constantly trying to create them by attempting to rescue my family from any possible difficulty, even if it meant living a mirage or lying to the people I loved most.

If only I could make them happy – then my world would be happy. If I could save them, maybe – just maybe – I could save me…

FORTY-FIVE

Our brain controls our decision-making, letting us know when to go forward with an action and when to stop. Scientists have learned which parts of the brain send these messages. And they know that for addicted people, these "stop" and "go" systems are impaired.

The brain's reward, or "go" system, is basic to all humans. Called the mesolimbic dopamine system, it evolved to help us pursue things necessary for survival such as food or sex. Conversely, the brain's frontal lobes or "stop" system evolved to help us weigh the consequences of our impulses. For example, this system will help keep us from driving through a red light when we're in a hurry, because the brain will tell us that doing so would be both dangerous and illegal. In this case, the "stop" system sends a message that the consequences of doing what the "go" system wants are too negative.

"When things are working right, the 'go' circuitry and the 'stop' circuitry really are interconnected and are really talking to each other to help you weigh the consequences of a decision and decide when to go or not to go," says Dr. Anna Rose Childress, a psychology researcher at the University of Pennsylvania. "It's not that they're separable. They're interactive. They're interlinked at all times." That means that even when you are in a great hurry and risk missing an appointment, you still do not run the red light. "Go" and "stop"

have communicated with each other, and "stop" has prevailed.

With Childress's addicted patients, however, "it is as though [the systems] have become functionally disconnected. It is as though the 'go' system is sort of running off on its own, is a rogue system now, and is not interacting in a regular, seamless, integrated way with the 'stop' system."

When an addicted person, even one who is working to recover, gets certain signs, or triggers, such as conflict with a companion, the "go" system overwhelms the part of the brain that's telling them, "Stop! This is a very bad idea!" The trigger can be something essential to the addicted person's life: one recovered writer realized that his addiction was partly triggered by the deadline pressure of his chosen profession as a journalist, and was prompted to start a new career; other recovering people often move from their old neighborhoods to be away from triggers. But a trigger can also be something as subtle as a scent that reminds a person of the place where they used to buy drugs.

When that trigger surfaces, Childress says, "instead of being able to say, 'What? Wait a minute. Think about what happened last week. You lost your job. You almost lost your life,' the 'stop' system doesn't seem to get into the picture at all. It's all about 'go.'"[31]

---

[31] HBO Addiction, Stop! Go! A Rogue System in the Brain

"Conner, honey, I know you're using again. You need to go back to rehab."

"I want to, Mom. I do. I have to. I can't live my life like this. I just want to feel good like I did when I came out before. I just want to be happy."

He stood in front of me looking even worse than the day he initially told me he was addicted to heroin. I looked into the eyes of my child. I knew he didn't know how to do this on his own. I saw a lost soul trapped in an addict's body. I knew that Conner wasn't the addict. The addict was someone else. How could I help him find himself again? What could I do for him?

Enabling is an incredibly powerful thing. It is born in insecurity. I can't "fix" myself, so I'll fix someone else. If I can be THAT powerful, then I'm in control of my life…

The thing is – Conner had to do this for himself.

I told him that I would give him the number to Bay Run – maybe they'd let him come back.

He wasn't sure they would.

Then again, he had finished the program. He had gotten his gold coin…

"Please, Mom, call for me. I'll go if they have a bed."

(What's the difference who calls, just so somebody does, right?)

"Okay. I'll call first thing in the morning."

"Do you think you can get a bed for Madison too?" (Madison?)

"I'll ask…"

FORTY-SIX

When my children were growing up they saw a lot of abuse. It's strange – it was so normal I don't think they were aware they were seeing something abnormal.

When Sam got angry he didn't just scream, or humiliate – he threw things! He turned tables over! He broke dishes, telephones, and other household items. Then he blamed someone else for making him so angry and wasting money because now those things needed to be fixed or replaced. He never took responsibility for his outbursts or tantrums. His violence was terrifying, and stressful.

My eldest daughter told me that she remembered a particular time when Sam was angry with Conner about something or other (it wasn't usually anything much), and he reached across the table, and punched him in the chest. The punch knocked Conner to the floor!

Sydney explained that (for her) it was horrifying!

There were other times, too, while growing up, that both girls would admit that they didn't need to worry if they made any mistakes because they knew Conner would get blamed for it anyway.

I did a lot of things right as I mother, and my heart was always in the right place. But I did all of my children an enormous disservice my brushing Sam's anger and constant displeasure under the rug.

There was one day, though, that I couldn't ignore or put behind me. It was a day that altered my viewpoint of my marriage, and who I was forever.

FORTY-SEVEN

January 12th, 2001. Most of the day was pretty normal. We went through our Saturday routine just as we always had. To be honest, I don't recall the details of the day at all.

In the evening, Sam and I decided to go down to the Irish Club a couple of blocks from our house. They were having a party that would include Irish Dancing, drinks and some small snack items.

We'd never been there before, but Sam thought it sounded like fun, and I figured, "why not?"

It was a warm, clear night with a comfortable breeze blowing, and all seemed right with the world. Conner was 18 years old, Sydney was 16, and Kim was 14. They were staying home for the evening.

Sam and I spent a couple of hours at the Irish Club. I had a couple of drinks (don't recall what, really), and Sam had several Irish Lagers. He seemed a bit drunk, but not bad. It was a fun night, and after a bit we drove the short distance to our house.

When we walked in the door, laughing and singing Sydney was sitting at the computer Instant Messaging with someone, Conner was up in his room playing a video game, and Kim was watching TV. As we walked in the door Sam was trying to remember the name to a song. I don't remember what song. I don't remember who the artist was.

He went over to the computer and said to Sydney, "Get off. I need to look something up."

Sydney minimized her Instant Message. "Okay, just a second Dad. I'm talking to someone. Let me tell them that I'll be back in a few minutes."

"NO!" he screamed, "Get off now!"

"I will," Sydney replied (a bit irritated). "I just want to tell Amy that I'll be right back."

He stood over her. The conversation she was really having was with a boy, and she was unwilling to maximize the IM while Sam was hovering over her.

"What are you trying to hide? This is MY computer, and MY house!" Sam's voice was very loud – very aggravated.

"Dad, I said I'd get off. Just let me tell her good-bye!"

"She doesn't need to hear good-bye! You don't need to tell her anything! What are you trying to hide? This is MY computer! Let me sit down!" And with that, he pushed the chair so Sydney would get up. She closed her IM window, and ran to her room with tears in her eyes.

Sam sat happily down at the computer to look up the name of the song.

I had gone up to the bathroom upon entering the house, and when I saw Sydney running up the stairs with tears in her eyes all I could think was, "now what?" Naturally, the fear that was so prevalent in our household when Sam got angry began to build within.

Conner had grown used to his father's anger, temper tantrums, and cruelty (well, as used to something like that as one can get). What Sam did to Sydney may not have been anywhere near as difficult, but for her – daddy's little princess who (to that point) could do no wrong – it was an enormous personal blow. It left her feeling confused and hurt.

Sydney and her father share the same kind of temperament in many ways. On top of feeling perplexed by what felt like an attack on her by her father, she was also feeling angry with him.

I went to see whether she was okay.

She was lying in her bed crying very hard. She kept telling me that she hadn't done anything wrong and asking why he was being so mean to her. I did the only thing I knew how to do – I made excuses for him.

Then I heard him call me from the bottom of the steps.

"What's going on up there? What are you doing?" He was screaming again...

"Sydney feels bad. I'm trying to help her feel better."

Ooops – wrong thing to say...

"SYDNEY feels bad? Why should Sydney feel bad? Why doesn't anyone care about how I feel? Why is EVERYONE more important than me?"

In that moment he started up the stairs, two at a time, and was heading for Sydney's room.

Sydney and Kim shared a bunk bed. Sydney slept in the top bunk. She was lying there holding her blanket (like a small child), giant alligator tears in her eyes, and as he approached her she backed as far away from him as she could. There was a look of terror in her eyes.

Kim was beneath. She had run to her bed as soon as Sam had started screaming.

"What do you think you're doing? I'm not the bad guy! You're nothing but a little slut!

What was it that was such a secret that you couldn't let me see? What are you doing? You whore!

"This is MY house – MY computer! What makes you think you can just use it whenever you want? I'm the important one! ME not YOU!"

Sydney screamed at him, "Stop!" and closed her eyes, crying hysterically.

"Sam, please – she's scared," I begged.

"SCARED? Scared of WHAT? Scared of this?" And he pounded his fist into her door breaking it into pieces. He continued to slam the doors to each bedroom. Our bedroom door has a full-length mirror on it that immediately was jarred loose, and crashed to the floor in a thousand pieces.

Conner had come out into the hallway when Sam was screaming.

"Dad…calm down…." Conner had always tried to understand his father's anger - to see his point of view. In retrospect, I think Conner felt sorry for his dad in a way. Conner had also become a bit of a peacemaker. He was always there to hold me when I was sad or frightened – especially when Sam's anger got the best of him. I believe that since we usually shared the brunt of his rage, he had come to feel my sadness, and the empathy he gave me had become innate.

"CALM DOWN! Why should I calm down?" My memory of Sam's face in that moment was one of complete fury – his eyes red, his whole body tense, and his voice almost horse from screaming...

He reached for Sydney, was attempting to hit her – punch her. She scooted back toward the wall as far as she could – curled up in a ball, crying. He couldn't reach her because of her position on the second level of the bunk bed.

I pleaded with him to stop.

"Fuck you all! I don't know why I put up with this! You treat me like a dog! You always turn me into the bad guy!! FUCK YOU!" And he went down the steps.

I tried to calm Sydney. I realized that we had to get out of there. All three of my children were in Sydney and Kim's room at this point.

"Pack a bag. Just throw some stuff in for a day or so. We've got to get out of here!"

"Are you sure, Mom?" Conner asked. I'm sure he was worried that Sam would be even angrier if we left, but I didn't see any choice. For the first time in my marriage I didn't believe any of us were safe. I had been frightened before, certainly, but I had never known him to be this violent and destructive. I felt certain that if we didn't leave it would only get worse.

The kids packed their small duffle bags, and we headed down the stairs. I remember feeling so frightened, but like a mother bear protecting her cubs, I led the way with all three children cowering behind me.

"WHERE do you think you are going? What the HELL are you doing?" As soon as he saw us, the anger rose up again.

"Sam, I think the kids need to go somewhere else tonight. You and I need to talk." I tried to sound brave, but I was petrified.

He practically growled. "So you're just going to leave then? Okay, fine!"

He picked up a small end table that he had made, and raised it over his head. It had been built with oak wood, and was heavy and strong. He hurled it at the floor. It didn't break right away. He picked it up several times throwing, and pounding it into the floor! Finally it began to weaken and broke into several small pieces.

The kids stood in shock, and fear in the entryway to our house.

"Sam, stop...." I was pleading with him.

"If you leave here. If these kids leave here, I won't be responsible for what you'll find tomorrow." He was threatening us. Calling us to fear what he might be capable of doing.

I didn't know what to do.

Should we leave? What would he do? Would he kill himself? Would he track us down, and do something to us?

At this point I wasn't sure, but I didn't want to take the chance…

"Go upstairs, "I said to them, "Stay in your rooms."

They ran up the steps.

He grabbed me by my shirt – in the front, and shook me back and forth until my shirt ripped. "You never liked that table anyway! WHY do you MAKE me do these things?"

He let go.

"I'll never be able to fix this table. Look what you made me do! You bitch. You fucking bitch!"

I wasn't aware of the drama that was happening upstairs while I tried to keep his temper at bay.

Sydney decided that she simply wasn't staying in the house. She told Conner that she was going to jump out the window, and leave!

Before anyone could stop her, she climbed out of her second story window, jumped onto a small back porch roof, clambered down into the yard, jumped the fence, and went across the street to a neighbor's house. When she got there – shaking and in tears – she called the police on her own father!

With the kids upstairs (or so he thought), and my having been put in my place, Sam began to calm down just a little. He picked up all the broken pieces of the table, and took them downstairs.

From behind me Conner quietly called my name.

"Sydney left. She jumped out the window."

"What? Is she okay?" I was so scared!

"Yeah, she went over to Kelvin's house. Mom, Kelvin says she called the police!"

"WHAT?" I tried to keep it at a whisper. "No…no…" I suppose I was frightened that he would even be angrier once he found out that his daughter had called the cops!

(Shit)

"You guys stay upstairs. He won't know she's gone…"

What could I do? I was trying desperately to formulate a plan to save my daughter from her father's rage. The police? Now what?

Very shortly – just after he came upstairs from the basement – we saw lights outside the house.

"What's that?" he asked with an angry concern.

I pretended I hadn't been expecting them. I looked out the door. "It's the police! Someone must have heard the screaming and called them."(We don't have air conditioning so in the middle of summer all the windows are all open).

"Great! Shit!" he said. "I have an interview with Chase University tomorrow. This is going to mess that up!"

(What?)

Two police officers came to the door. I let them in.

"What's going on here tonight folks?"

"Nothing, really." Sam said.

"Nothing? Well, there must be something," one officer replied." We received a call about loud arguing. Everything okay?"

"Everything's fine," Sam answered.

The police officers looked at me.

I was sobbing quietly – exhausted, frightened, and confused...

"What do you want us to do?" (Did he want to know if I wanted to press charges? Was he kidding? Sam would really be pissed if I had him taken off to jail!)

"I don't know...."

The officers were silent for a moment. They looked at Sam. They looked at me. "What would you like to happen here, Ma'am?"

"I just want him to stop screaming...." And I broke out in loud, uncontrolled sobs. "I just want him to stop yelling..."

The two officers turned toward Sam. "Is that possible, sir? Can you just stop yelling?"

"What are you doin' - surrounding me?" Sam replied rather sarcastically.

"No, sir - we're not surrounding you. We're just asking if you can stop screaming. Can't you see your wife is frightened?"

Sam looked at me, and then to the officers. "Yeah, I can handle that."

To be honest – in that moment – I really wanted them to take him away. I wanted to escape. But I was far too frightened. I must have looked like a crumpled mess sitting on the sofa. Thinking back on what the officers must have been looking at is quite revealing.

They saw a man far too quick to answer, his wife sitting sniveling on the sofa with a torn shirt, and their daughter across the street having called the police. It's no wonder that they asked me to step outside.

"Mr. Jobes, please take some time to calm down. We don't want to have to come back out here. Is that possible?"

"Yeah, I'm fine. (YOU'RE FINE?) Everything's fine." It is?) Sam said. He moved past them, and went upstairs.

I called the kids down. I asked Conner to go over to Kelvin's house and get Sydney.

"Are you going to be okay?" one police officer asked.

"Yes, I think so." I said.

"Do you need us to call a battered women's shelter?"

I was surprised. "No...no.... I'm sure he's fine now."

"Ma'am," the other police officer started, "do you know if he has a gun in the house?"

(A gun? Did they think he might shoot me – or himself? Would he?) I don't think I was sure at that time...

"Well, yes...he has a couple. But I don't think you have to worry about that."

"Are you sure? These things can escalate sometimes."

"No, no...it's fine." I guess I sort of believed it.

They told me to call them if I needed their assistance again – reminding me that I could always go to a women's shelter if necessary...

They left.

Somewhere in that time frame (I don't recall when), my neighbor, Jackie, stopped over.

I guess she saw the police cars...

"Jackie, can the kids stay with you tonight? I need to talk to Sam. We had a little trouble tonight."

She seemed concerned (I guess she saw the torn shirt too). 'Did I need help?' 'Was I going to be okay?' (No, really, I'm...fine?)

The kids walked slowly to her house with their duffle bags.

I went back into the house – unsure of what was to transpire, but hoping he wouldn't get so angry again…

FORTY-EIGHT

Sam was in the attic. I don't know why or what he was doing (hopefully he wasn't getting his shotgun), but I knew that we had to talk.

The idea of having a real dialogue with Sam was almost pathetic. We hadn't experienced that kind of communication in the thirty years I'd known him. To imagine that he'd suddenly be open to sitting down and sharing thoughts and feelings about the situation that had just transpired had me wondering if there was any hope at all for us to resolve anything.

Still, I felt I had to try. I am a communicator - not a fighter. It would be up to me to initiate any conversation, and to direct it onto a positive, meaningful course.

When I got to the top of the steps Sam was just coming down the ladder that lifted into the attic. He gave me an angry, hateful look.

"I think we should try to talk…"

"Talk about what, Anne? What is there to talk about?" He was still really angry, and I was still really scared.

"Honey, I really think…"

"Don't HONEY me! That's bullshit! If you cared about me at all you wouldn't have taken

Sydney's side. None of this would have happened!" (It was my fault)

"She was frightened…"

"Frightened of what? WHAT did I do that was so bad? Did I hit her?" (No, but only because you couldn't reach her) "Did I hurt ANYONE? What did you think was going to happen?"

He wasn't yelling – he was barking through clenched teeth in a deep, heated voice.

"I don't know what I thought was going to happen, but you were really angry, and I don't think it's good for the kids to see you so out of control…"

"Out of control? OUT OF CONTROL? HOW else am I supposed to act when you all gang up on me like that? If you would EVER take my side it would be a miracle. YOU have them all against me! This is MY house! WHY should I be the one to have to go through this?"

It was clear I wasn't getting through to him.

He marched down the stairs.

I followed him like a puppy dog hoping to be thrown a bone.

For the next twenty minutes or so we cleaned up around the house. It's odd how "normal" activity can calm someone a bit. I guess (without thought) we were both just trying to let go of things a bit.

He didn't say he was going to bed. He didn't ask where the kids were. He didn't ask what the police had said to me. He just turned out the lights and went upstairs.

I stood in the dark for a minute wondering what I was going to do – speculating on my own future, and the expectations I might have for my children.

I went into the bedroom, changed my clothes, and climbed into bed.

"Sam, please talk to me," I begged.

"Anne, I don't know what there is to talk about..."

For the next four hours I tried to talk to him. I tried to explain to him why his anger frightened me so much. I tried to help him understand that our children needed to feel secure and safe. I tried to make it sound as if we both needed to do a much better job with that (which was true).

For the next four hours Sam turned everything around to me. He put our children down – telling me that they were all "waste material." He told me as calm and cool as he's ever been that he was sorry he had married me and sorry that the kids had ever been born – that he could have been so much happier if he'd never have met me. He blamed me for everything that he's ever done that was negative.

I tried to explain some things from my past that he didn't understand, that he didn't even know about. I tried to tell him why I was so frightened, and why I didn't want the kids to feel this way.

It's difficult to explain what it was that I was feeling in those long hours that I tried to talk to him. I felt completely defeated. I was crushed. I was concerned. I was confused. I was exhausted. I cried myself to sleep just as the sun was beginning to rise on the horizon.

From that night on, nothing was really ever the same again.

FORTY-NINE

It was the 7th of April 2007 – the day before Easter.

"Bay Run admissions, this is Sally."

"Hi, Sally!"(A familiar voice) "My name is Anne Jobes. My son Conner was just released from Bay Run about a month ago. He's using again, and would like to come back. Would that be possible? Do you have an open bed in detox?"

"You say he finished the program?"

"Yes, he finished. He got his gold coin." I said proudly. "But he didn't go the halfway house, and he needs to come back…"

"Well, Anne, usually once a patient has been through our system we usually try to place him somewhere else since it's possible they might approach him in another way – one that might be more helpful for his personality."

That sounded reasonable, but Conner really liked Bay Run. I don't know if he'd agree to go somewhere else. I told her what I thought.

"Okay. Well, since he did make it through the whole program… You say it's been a month? Let me see if we can let him come back here again. We do have an bed open…"

(Please....)

After a few minutes she came back onto the line and told me that they would be able to pick him up today. "He'll have to call himself though…"

"Oh, yes…yes…. I'll call him now…thank you so much!" (Today!! He's going back today!)

And then I remembered Madison.

"Oh, Conner asked me to ask you – he has a friend who wants to come too. Is it possible that you might have a bed for her?"

Sally explained to me that, although they might have a bed, they don't like to put friends in the same facility. It doesn't usually help either of them – especially if they've used together in the past.

"We don't condone the continuance of a relationship between two addicts. Have her call Rosy Glenn Rehab. If they have a bed, they can pick her up."

I decided to call Rosy Glenn because I wanted to be sure and give Conner as much good information as possible. If Madison going to rehab would help Conner to go, I was willing to do whatever was necessary.

Calling Rosy Glenn was painless. The associate on the other line was very nice, and confirmed that they had a bed. The problem was – Madison was still only 17 years old. She wouldn't be 18 (and an adult) for another week. If they admitted her to the children's unit she would have to stay in the children's unit.

Okay...

I called Conner. I told him that they could pick him up today – around 1:30pm (it was already 12:30pm, and the driver happened to already be in our area). I told him that he had to call them. Then I told him what Rosy Glenn had told me about Madison. He was fine with that. He told me he'd call them, and then give Madison Rosy Glenn's number.

"I don't want to be sick, Mom, and I haven't had anything today. Do you think they'll give me something so I don't have to be sick?"

"I'll check with them. I'm sure they'll give you something." I had NO idea if they'd give him something, but I wasn't going to let his being dope sick stop him from the opportunity for recovery!

I remember waiting by the phone for his call as if my life depended on it too. It had very much become my opportunity for recovery – my survival. Every emotion within me was afire! I was hopeful, frightened, unsure, confident, nervous, excited, and mostly impatient. WHY didn't he call me back? WHAT was taking so long?

The phone rang.

FINALLY!

"Mom, Bay Run is going to pick me up at 1:30pm, but Madison doesn't want to be in the children's unit so Rosy Glenn can't pick her up until next week." (I could hear Madison crying in the background).

"It's okay, Honey," I said to him. "I'll make sure and do everything I can to help her."

I could hear her begging Conner to wait to go until she could go too. I heard her saying that she wanted to be where Conner was. He kept trying to talk to me, but she was wailing in the background.

I felt sorry for her, but at that point in my life I didn't care about her at all. I just wanted Conner to be okay.

"Conner, let me talk to Madison."

He handed the phone to her.

"Hello?" she said with a broken voice.

"Madison, listen to me. Do you love Conner?"

"Yes…"

"Then you have to let him go." (It was almost 1:30pm already – the driver would be there any time now). "Madison, if you love him, you have to let him walk out that door.

You want him to get better, right?"

"Yes…but I don't want to be alone…." She sobbed.

I really felt for her – she'd just lost her mother to cancer a few months ago, but my son needed to be in recovery. I had blinders on!

"Madison, listen to me. Are you listening? I will do everything I can to help you. You won't be alone. I won't let you fail. I will make sure you get a bed. I'll help you when you're there. Whatever you need. I will be there for you. I promise, Honey. But you have to let Conner go today. There's a bed today. Do you understand?"

"Yes…."

"Please, Madison. Just let him go today." I begged her (hoping her insecure, distorted, obsessed heart and mind could find the compassion it might take to wish him well).

"Okay…."

Conner got back on the phone.

"Conner, get your stuff together. I'll send what you don't have."

"Mom," Conner was whispering, "I don't think she's going to let me go. She's crying, and begging me not to leave her. I can't stand it. I feel so bad…" He sounded desperate.

"Conner I will help her. I promise you, Honey, I will do whatever it takes. I won't let her be alone. I told her all of this already. I won't let her fall in between the cracks. I'll take care of her, but you have to take care of you right now, Conner. The driver's going to be at the door any second."

"I know," he said. "Mom, you'll make sure she gets into rehab? You promise?"

"Yes, I promise, Conner. Call me when the driver's outside, okay? Get your stuff…"

Within ten minutes my phone was ringing, and Conner said that the driver was out front. I already knew he was there because I had (somehow) gotten the driver's cell phone number, and called him. I wanted to warn him that Madison might come running out after Conner. "Don't let her talk him out of it!" I had pleaded with him.

"Mom, you're going to help Madison, right? Please promise me you'll help her too…" I could hear Madison crying, and begging Conner not to leave her. At that point in time I would have done almost ANYTHING to get him into the van!

"I promise, Conner. Tell Madison I'll call her tomorrow. Just get on the van, Honey, please."

"Are they going to give me something so I don't have to be sick?" (Shit)

"Yes, Conner. I spoke with the detox nurse, and she said that the doctor would write something for you tonight." I lied through my teeth.

"Okay, Mom...I'll call you when I can."

Within one minute I was back on the phone with John (the Bay Run transportation driver). I wanted to be sure that Conner had gotten into the van.

"John?"

"It's me Mom."

"Conner?" He was on John's phone! "How did you answer this phone?"

"As soon as he saw your number he handed it over to me."

"Oh.... good...well, you're in the van now, then?" I was so hopeful...

"Yes, Mom. I'm in the van."

"Have you pulled away from Madison's house? She's not running after the van, is she?" (Please let him get away from there!)

"Yes, Mom – we're at the end of the street. I'm okay." He sounded glad to be in the van too.

"Okay, Honey. I love you so much. I'm so proud of you… Call me when you can, okay?"

"I will. I love you too… They are going to give me something, right?" He was still frightened about feeling dope sick.

"I told you they would, Baby…"

"Okay."

"Put John back on." I needed to be sure that they were moving further and further away and that Madison wasn't running desperately after them.

He assured me that they were on the road, and that no one was running after them. He told me that Conner was fine, and would be at Bay Run in time for dinner (if he was able to eat).

I thanked him, and hung the phone up.

Okay…

Okay.

FIFTY

It was Easter time. Each holiday in our family is celebrated by either going to my sister-in-law's house, my husband's niece's house or staying at our house, and having the whole group of them come to us.

This particular Easter it was our turn to cook.

Along with the "regular" family members who were coming to eat, my sister-in-law's youngest child, Ken, who was in the Air Force and not usually in Portersville for the holiday was also visiting with his wife and two sons.

Although other family members oftentimes make excuses for Ken, in my opinion Ken is a controlling, abusive, know-it-all with a loud mouth, and cruel eyes. I don't like him. I don't respect him at all.

But – he's family – Sam's family – and we set a place for him.

As people started to arrive, Sam welcomed them as Kim and I continued the finishing touches on the meal. When it was time to carve the turkey, Kim and I played hostesses while Sam carved. The conversation was superficial (at best), which is normal for Sam's family. We chitchatted about nothing.

When I considered what that last few months of my life had been like, it was difficult to even care who the best singer was on American Idol or how much the price of lettuce had gone up.

When it was time to eat I was relieved. The sooner we ate, the sooner they would be leaving.

Ken's boys sat at a separate smaller table with Sam's great-niece, Lucy, and our daughter Kim.

Again – the chitchatting…

Then someone asked how Conner was. I don't know how much they really cared. I knew they didn't understand. I knew Sam didn't understand. As far as they were concerned, Conner was a fuck-up. They didn't say it right out, but the comments and questions made it obvious.

In a way, I couldn't blame them.

There are a lot of stigmas attached to addiction. I didn't understand it either (before I became so entangled with it myself):

Myths About Addiction

- *1. Addicts are bad, crazy, or stupid.*
- *Evolving research is demonstrating that addicts are not bad people who need to get good, crazy people who need to get sane, or stupid people who need education.*

Addicts have a brain disease that goes beyond their use of drugs.
- *2. Addiction is a willpower problem.*
- *This is an old belief, probably based upon wanting to blame addicts for using drugs to excess. This myth is reinforced by the observation that most treatments for alcoholism and addiction are behavioral (talk) therapies, which are perceived to build self-control. But addiction occurs in an area of the brain called the mesolimbic dopamine system that is not under conscious control.*
- *3. Addicts should be punished, not treated, for using drugs.*
- *Science is demonstrating that addicts have a brain disease that causes them to have impaired control over their use of drugs. Addicts need treatment for their neurochemically driven brain pathology.*
- *4. People addicted to one drug are addicted to all drugs.*
- *While this sometimes occurs, most people who are dependent on a drug may be dependent on one or two drugs, but not all. This is probably due to how each drug "matches up" with the person's brain chemistry.*
- *5. Addicts cannot be treated with medications.*
- *Actually, addicts are medically detoxified in hospitals, when appropriate, all the time. But can they be treated with*

medications after detox? New pharmacotherapies (medicines) are being developed to help patients who have already become abstinent to further curb their craving for addicting drugs. These medications reduce the chances of relapse and enhance the effectiveness of existing behavioral (talk) therapies.

- *6. Addiction is treated behaviorally, so it must be a behavioral problem.*
- *New brain scan studies are showing that behavioral treatments (i.e., psychotherapy) and medications work similarly in changing brain function. So addiction is a brain disease that can be treated by changing brain function, through several types of treatments.*
- *7. Alcoholics can stop drinking simply by attending AA meetings, so they can't have a brain disease.*

The key word here is "simply." For most people, AA is a tough, lifelong working of the Twelve Steps. On the basis of research, we know that this support system of people with a common experience is one of the active ingredients of recovery in AA. AA doesn't work for everyone, even for many people who truly want to stop drinking.[32]

---

[32] * Adapted from Myths of Addiction. Carlton K. Erickson, Ph.D., University of Texas Addiction Science

After the ignorant comments about how Conner should "straighten up his life" or the questions about "why" he would do "something like this" we were told (by Ken) how a "good" parent raises their child so that these kinds of things would never become an issue. He continued on about how beating and controlling their every move was the way to go (he's always been the perfect example of an abusive father).

We were also fortunate enough to hear the kids (Ken's boys, and Sam's great-niece, Lucy) snickering at the small table when one of them sarcastically asked, "Where's Conner?" Kim told me later that they were kicking one another knowingly under the table, and then giggling, as if they had been told ahead of time not to let anyone hear them discussing the matter.

It's fascinating how defensive I felt – natural too, I suppose...

I really couldn't wait for them all to just go home!

FIFTY-ONE

Conner went back into detox on Saturday, April 7th, 2007. The following Saturday I received a call from Josh (Madison's sister's boyfriend) who told me that Conner's car was parked on the street nearby, and that it was parked illegally – that he was going to begin to get a lot of tickets if it didn't get moved.

Conner had locked the keys to his car inside the glove compartment when he was preparing to leave for Bay Run a few days before. (No one wanted Madison's family to have any control on the car again). Fortunately, we had a spare key.

I explained the situation to Sam. The original plan was to drive it back to our house for now, but when we arrived at its location that evening we were struck with yet another issue: two of Conner's tires had been slashed, and both of his mirrors were broken off (of course they were).

We weren't driving this car anywhere!

After a very heated deliberation, we decided to call AAA and ask them to drop it off at Dylan's Tire Service not far from where it was parked. We'd have the tires replaced, and then Sam could fix the mirrors.

AAA came after about an hour of waiting, but the truck they brought was not the type that could haul a car with two flat tires. Again, we discussed our options (this time with the driver), and we ended up giving him the keys to the car. He called another truck, and waited for it so it could be towed to Dylan's.

As we drove home Sam complained about having to have wasted his whole evening – it shouldn't have been necessary if Conner had any brains in his head….

But, you know, at least Sam had gone and done it with me. It was one of the first things I hadn't had to do on my own. And Conner was in recovery.

Conner was in recovery.

I felt very, very hopeful.

FIFTY-TWO

In the two years that followed the incident in January of 2001 we all went through enormous changes.

Conner had been diagnosed with ADD, and had gone into a temporary remission with his Rheumatoid Arthritis. This meant that he was not taking his Methotrexate any longer. This also meant that he could drink alcohol now. I was concerned. Little did I know he had already started down the road of drug abuse, which eventually led to his heroin addiction.

Sydney went into a deep depression. She reacted to her father's abuse that night by disrespecting herself. She began to drink, and smoke weed. She became sexually active. Her relationship was far more strained as far as her father was concerned. He began to find all manner of things wrong with how she dressed, how she spoke, what she did, and the like. By the following July Sydney told me that she needed help – she wanted to see a therapist.

Kim seemed to have gone into some kind of denial. It was as if what had happened wasn't all that bad. To this day, even though she's aware that his behavior that evening was over-the-top, she doesn't consider it all that unusual – "people get mad all the time." My belief is that she became used to the anger and that (given her personality) she rejected the fear (or at least, redirected it into other areas of her life). It's far more comfy to think there's nothing wrong with someone who would act like that when you love them so deeply. I have come to respect her unconditional love for him.

The fact is - all of us love him in our own ways.

We have all come to see his strengths.

We have all come to understand his vulnerabilities.

He makes us laugh as often as he irritates us.

He still gets angry - I am just not afraid any longer.

There is balance more often these days.

But in July of 2002 we were still feeling the shockwaves of that terrible night the previous January. In our own ways we had not really made sense of it. For a long time afterwards I wasn't even able to talk about it. I felt almost numb. I believe now that I just didn't know what to feel. I was simply too confused…

I made an appointment with Jessica Day – a family therapist at Somerset Family Health Services. I decided that all of us needed to work through our feelings so that we might let go of any negativity that had been ignited that night.

I had discussed our all going with Sam, but he practically ordered us not to go – that nothing was wrong with him – that WE were the ones with the problems and no "shrink" was going to fix us. I was told not to waste the money!

I went against his wishes.

We went anyway.

FIFTY-THREE

Jessica Day was a quirky kind of person, but over the course of the next six months while we worked through our issues with her, we grew to depend on her quite a bit. The therapies that each of us experienced were slightly different dependent on our individual needs and our willingness to work through our fear.

After the first two meetings Kim decided she did not want to partake in any more of the sessions. I think now that by participating (for her) it was as if she were admitting that her father had done something wrong. She was not willing to accept his shortcomings in that way.

Although I have come to believe that some of what Kim saw and heard growing up has affected her deeply, I've also come to see her use much of what she experienced as a natural tool to become a strong, confident woman.

Jessica worked with us individually, and as a group. We talked a lot about the event in January of 2001, but we also talked a lot about many of the things that had occurred over the kids' lifetimes. Perhaps those sessions helped us to better understand Sam's limitations, but more importantly (I think) our own reactions to his behavior. We better understood ourselves, and the dynamics that had created how codependent we had become with one another.

Jessica also told us that we were suffering from Post Traumatic Stress Disorder. *Post-traumatic stress disorder is a type of anxiety disorder that's triggered by an extremely traumatic event. You can develop post-traumatic stress disorder (PTSD) when a traumatic event happens to you or when you see a traumatic event happen to someone else.*[33]

---

[33] Post Traumatic Stress Disorder (PSDS), MayoClinic.com
*EMDR is a new controversial form of therapy; Francine Shapiro Ph.D developed it in 1987. Dr. Shapiro was in a park and was thinking about some unpleasant memories. She noticed that when she moved her eyes back and forth that the intensity of the negative emotions of these unpleasant memories seemed to dissipate. This incident was followed by intense studies and in 1989, Dr. Shapiro reported that she was having success-using EMDR to treat trauma. During EMDR sessions, the therapist asks the client to think about a traumatic event and at the same time, move their eyes rapidly - following the movement of a pencil or a finger by the therapist. It has been learned that painful or traumatic experiences are stored in a different place in the brain than are pleasant or neutral ones. Normally we work through these negative experiences by talking about it, dreaming about it, etc. We are able to put it behind us. However many traumatic experiences seem to be "stuck" in the brain. Even after years of talk therapy, the intensity of painful feelings about a particular trauma could remain the same without change. Some people feel that EMDR is able to "un-stick" these experiences so that it reconnects with the healthy brain and then is reprocessed and integrated at an accelerated speed. The theory is that the rapid eye movement in EMDR creates similar brain activity to REM (rapid eye movement) that we experience during sleep. This REM assists us in processing ideas and resolves conflicts. We are able to work through things. We still retain the memory but without the emotional pain and the feelings of smell, taste, etc. of the event. –EMDR:

She suggested that we try a rather controversial new therapy called Eye Movement Desensitization and Reprocessing or *EMDR*.* Naturally, we were open to anything that might make us feel better, and help us to move on with our lives.

I can't speak for Conner or Sydney directly, but I can say that the EMDR treatment I received really made an enormous difference! I was able to recall the details of January 12th without feeling any of the emotional reactions to those details.

For me, what it actually did was allow me to distance myself from the emotion so I would more clearly be able to access my situation.

In private therapy I also became aware for the first time that Sam was a "batterer." As I mentioned in an earlier chapter, I really had no idea that "battery" could be emotional or verbal. Until that point I thought it meant physical abuse – hitting, etc., as my mother had done in addition to the emotional abuse.

It allowed me (for the first time) to recognize that his anger was not my fault; that I hadn't been doing something wrong; that I wasn't responsible for his happiness. It was the first time I allowed

---

Treatment Option for Post Traumatic Stress Disorder by Patty Pheil M.S.W.

my husband to take responsibly for his own actions (even if he would never do that himself).

It was the beginning of an intense kind of freedom that I had never known. I was beginning to see my own strength.

Conner only met with Jessica Day a half a dozen times or so. Looking back, I think he probably needed far more therapy than any of us, but (at the time) he felt that he was okay. Even if I should have, I didn't force him to continue going.

Sydney, on the other hand, was the one who had suggested it, and who was able to recognize her own deep need to work through the intense feelings that she was having.

She was angry.

And she had gotten mean.

She was taking it out on herself, on everyone around her, but especially on me (at least from my perspective). I sometimes wondered if she weren't angry with me for letting her father get away with so much over the years. Why hadn't I had more of a backbone?

It wasn't until a couple of years later in private therapy once again that I would finally figure out that I had lived in fear of emotional and physical abandonment all of my life – that disagreeing or standing up for myself only meant that I would be somehow threatened. I lived in such trepidation that I hadn't been able to stand up to Sam – even for the sake of my own children...

In the late summer of 2002 Jessica suggested that Sydney and I spend more one-on-one time together to work through our issues. Honestly, I'm not sure if we had a real handle on what those issues were, but it didn't matter, really. After several weeks of spending time together – going out to lunch – or whatever, we began to reconnect once again. After several months had passed we were much closer, and the trust we had once shared had returned.

Thinking about it now, I realize that Jessica Day was a very good therapist. Had we had more time with her (especially Conner) who knows how different things might have been!

Although my relationship with Sydney was beginning to flourish once again, she was still very depressed. While she hadn't been interested in medications previously, after about six months worth of therapy she decided that she'd give antidepressants a try. So, for about a year after we stopped seeing Jessica, Sydney used the anti-depressant, *Celexa*. [34]

---

[34] Celexa is an antidepressant in a group of rugs called selective serotonin reuptake inhibitors (SSRIs). It works by restoring the balance of serotonin, a natural occurring substance found in the brain, which

Within two weeks of starting the medication she was a new person! My Sydney had returned to me!

The year following her therapy (although they had been close beforehand), Sydney and Conner began to develop an even closer relationship. In many ways they were best friends. They partied together, snuck out in the middle of the night together, shared many of the same friends, and talked. Sydney was, in many ways, Conner's therapist. She understood him. She knew what he'd been through. Her experiences offered him a certain kind of hope. She had become his closest comrade in arms.

Taking all of that into consideration, I believe that Sydney's leaving for the Army had a deep effect on Conner, and that with everything else he had going on (internally) it was (at least in part) a catalyst for his slow, downward spiral.

---

helps to improve certain mood problems. Celexa is used to treat depression.

FIFTY-FOUR

The two weeks following Conner's re-admittance to Bay Run had been incredible for me. New hope had arisen in my heart, and I was sleeping peacefully knowing that he was safe.

I had worked with Madison for a week after Conner had gone back into rehab, and finally helped her be admitted to Rosy Glenn. I sent her a few necessities to ease her transition. I fulfilled my promise.

With the summer coming, I knew that my son might not make it back home to enjoy it with us, so I was eager to visit, and see with my own eyes how he was doing.

Bay Run Rehabilitation Services hosts something called, "Loved One's Day" each Saturday. The first time Conner was at Bay Run he never really mentioned Loved One's Day. This time around, he called us about two weeks after he was in rehab and asked us if we were going to attend.

His whole attitude now seemed very different. He appeared cautious about his own recovery. He wanted it more than ever, but he was far too aware that relapse was easy. Although he was feeling physically better as each day passed, he was not over confident this time. He knew that the road ahead of him was a long one. He was aware of his own vulnerability.

Conner thought it was possible that he would be at Bay Run this time for 28 days. But additionally, he was strongly considering going to a halfway house this time. *The Half way Houses are to assist men and women in preventing relapse, developing the skills and self-motivation they need to successfully adjust to a drug-free lifestyle and to maintain it after they leave the facility. The clients receive daily instruction and practice skills in the development of positive life goals and responsibilities.*[35] He told us that he'd talk to us more about it when we came up to visit on Loved One's Day.

I wasn't sure Sam would want to go, but then again, he felt it was simply a visit - not a lecture. To be honest, I think he too, needed to see how Conner was doing.

We stayed at a motel in Hinesboro (just outside of Wallingburg, RI) on Friday evening since we had to be at the rehab facility by 8am in the morning.

After a continental breakfast we drove the 30-minute drive toward Aylesboro, on to Wallingburg, and eventually arrived at Bay Run around 7:45am.

---

[35] © 2004-2009 CRC Health Group, Inc., Cove Forge, White Deer Run

We were led to a large room filled with tables and chairs. They had set-up coffee and donuts for the guests. I gave them a few things for Conner (unwrapped, of course, since they would have to go through them for contraband or anything that wasn't acceptable for an addict in treatment).

We sat at the end of one of the tables, and about ten minutes later Conner arrived. He looked good - much healthier. But I sensed a guarded attitude that I hadn't seen when he had been home from Bay Run those first few days in November. It was so good to wrap my arms around him. Then he leaned in, and hugged his father.

(This is very, very good)

Shortly, a kindly gentleman named Daniel welcomed all of us, and began an instruction on addiction, recovery, and enabling. He told us stories of his own addiction, and recovery - of relapse - and of embracing the *twelve-step program*.[36]

---

[36] A twelve-step program is a set of guiding principles outlining a course of action for recovery from addiction, compulsion, or other behavioral problems. Originally proposed by Alcoholics Anonymous (AA) as a method of recovery from alcoholism, the Twelve Steps were first published in the book, *Alcoholics Anonymous: The Story of How More Than One Hundred Men Have Recovered From Alcoholism* in 1939. The method was then adapted and became the foundation of other twelve-step programs such as Narcotics Anonymous, Overeaters Anonymous, Co-Dependents Anonymous and Debtors Anonymous. The process of twelve-step recovery has been characterized by Dr.

He told us what "our addict's" days were like at Bay Run, what was expected of them, and what they needed to expect from themselves.

He often asked questions of the family, and brought the eleven recovering addicts who were in attendance into the conversation. He was honest, funny, and encouraging. But he warned us too, that addiction is a disease fraught with setbacks, and responses born in conditions. He reminded us that *addicted people must learn how to avoid contact with the triggers that may set in motion their brain's demanding cry for drugs or alcohol. And when those triggers are unavoidable, people must develop the skills that will prevent the craving from taking over. Learning these skills must be a core element of any treatment program; maintaining them should be part of an aftercare program or long-term recovery plan.*[37]

We all took a break around 11am and ate lunch in the cafeteria. The food wasn't bad. It was institutional food, but acceptable enough.

After lunch, Daniel led us down a much more personal road.

We talked about enabling. He gave us lists of "excuses" our addicts would give to us. He told us

---

Bob - one of AA's co-founders - as "Trust God, clean house, help others".

[37] Avoiding Relapse, HBO Addiction

how they would lie to us. He told us that we would lie to ourselves, and to one another.

In turn each family told their story of addiction. The tales were heart retching. Mothers, fathers, sisters, husbands, wives, and other family members chronicled the addiction, the fear, and the confusion of sometimes years, and years of codependence. Some of them had lost everything they owned to alcohol. One man was on the verge of divorce because of cocaine use. Another had lost so many jobs he didn't feel that he was any longer employable.

One particular person struck me more empathetically than any of the others - a beautiful 19-year-old girl who was addicted to cocaine and heroin, and had been using since she was 15 years old. Her mother's eyes were filled with tears. Her father seemed despairingly desperate. The young girl sat there - very aware of her compulsion - but also unsure of her own ability to be successful at recovery.

Nineteen years old...

We went around the room speaking to one another. Conner, along with the other patients at Bay Run, was told to tell their loved ones one thing that they had lied to us about. Conner told us that he had taken far more drugs than we had known about all these years, and that heroin wasn't the first thing he had been addicted to.

We, in turn, were supposed to tell one another something we had lied about. Daniel explained that lying is an additive behavior, and that family members often unconsciously take on some of the same habits.

"I lied when I told you that you were going to get something to make you feel better the day they picked you up to come out here again," I said to Conner.

I turned to Sam. "I lied to you about what Conner was really taking."

Sam looked at both of us and said, "I never lied about anything."

I knew it was true, and I respected him deeply in that moment. At the same time I felt even more alone. I felt like he would never have understood why I felt a need to lie. He wasn't really aware of what it felt like to be afraid...

In the closing Love One's Day exercise at Bay Run that day we were instructed to tell our addicts what would happen if they came home and began using again. The addict was not permitted to speak or make a comment in return.

Daniel (the facilitator) started at the opposite end of the table from where we sat. As we moved slowly around the room - after having learned all that we had learned that day - family members were quite obviously feeling much stronger and more knowledgeable about their own options as far as their loved one's addictions were concerned. We all felt a sense of needing to take control of something that had been out of control for so long.

As people spoke to their own addicts in the room, we all listened with tears in our eyes. The pain in the room was palpable - we were hearing their pain, and feeling our own. The fear of losing their loved ones, the confusion of their addict's choices, and the hope that a new beginning would be possible were obvious as well.

There were many promises that if the addict didn't stop, they would no longer be permitted into the house, or the spouse left behind would take the children away, or that they'd never be spoken to again.

I remember thinking that some of these people didn't really "get" the facts. *Addiction is a disease. Families must have a realistic understanding of what to expect from treatment, since there is no cure for this disease. The idea is to manage the disease, the way diabetes is managed. But there may be relapses, as there are with any other chronic illness.*[38] I thought that some of the things they said to their loved ones was rather harsh, to be honest.

Of course, this was a sign that I was still codependent. It had turned into my addiction on

---

[38] HBO Addiction, "Why Can't They Just Stop?"

an emotional level. I was making excuses for my son. In my mind I knew the facts. I understood the "idea" of enabling. But outwardly, I knew better. I was justifying his choices, and my own behavior. I wanted to be the pillow he would land on if he fell. I didn't want him to get hurt. I wanted to "save" him. (I wanted to save myself). I remember thinking that I understood addiction better than almost anyone in the room…

Finally, it was our turn to tell Conner what we would do if he came back home, and started using again. We were the last ones to speak.

I looked into my son's eyes. He was obviously already deeply moved by the words of the other family members in the room. His own guilt was tangible to me. He told me in that one single moment – within his gaze – how sorry he was for everything…

"Conner," I began – my voice cracking with emotion. "You have always been my rock. It's you I've turned to when I was sad. You held me, and made me feel safe. I depended on you. I love you more than I will ever be able to express…"

Tears stung my eyes.

Conner was crying too.

"But if you come home, and start using again, you'll have to leave. I can't let you stay there. I can't watch you kill yourself any more. I can't give you money…" I was sobbing.

"And you have to stay away from those people!" (I meant Madison, and her family. He knew whom I was referring to). "You just have to…"

Conner nodded at me, wiping a tear from his face.

"I love you so much. No matter what you do I will always love you. But I can't help you to kill yourself…"

I touched his face. He mouthed the words, "I know…"

Now it was Sam's turn. Conner's father hadn't said many positive things to him over the years. He hadn't really encouraged him genuinely – only critically. I'm sure neither of them could remember the last time they had told one another that they loved each other.

I also knew that Sam's words in the next few minutes were very important. The one thing Conner has always needed was his father's approval and love. I've tried to tell Sam over the years that if he could find a way to express these things to Conner, it would make a world of difference. Sam always thought I was full of "shit" – that he had done everything he could for Conner – that Conner just "didn't care".

I suppose sometimes (maybe most of the time) we don't really see what we're doing or saying to others. But I knew that this moment was critical for both of them.

Sam's eyes were filled with tears. It had been a long day. (It had been a long couple of months).

"Conner, if you keep doing this shit you're going to die. Do you understand that? You're going to die. I know people who do this kind of thing. I know what I'm talking about."

His eyes filled with more tears. One spilled over and ran down his face.

"I haven't kicked you out because your mother begged me not to. If you come home and you do this shit again, you will be OUT! You're mother is right – you can't hang out with any of those people anymore! You've got to stop!"

Another tear. A pause.

"I'm not kidding, Conner." He seemed to be finished, and then, "I love you."

My heart felt a deep gratitude. I looked at Conner. He was crying. And although the addicts were not supposed to speak, Conner said out loud, "I love you too, Dad."

It was one of the most incredible moments of my life.

A corner had been turned.

FIFTY-FIVE

In the five years following our EMDR treatments with Jessica Day until Loved One's Day at Bay Run I had moved through a slow process of renewal in many ways. It was a long, pain-staking route, to be sure.

In that time I found an ability to forgive myself for all the things I had believed for so long that I had been doing wrong. I wasn't able to make my mother happy (no matter how I tried for so many years in every way imaginable). I wasn't able to make my husband happy. I wasn't able to fix anything, really. There had been an enormous remorse in that for me. The more I tried, the more I failed, and the worse I had felt about myself.

Now I was beginning to feel the wings of freedom! It isn't that I didn't want the people in my life to be happy, but I became deeply aware that I was unable to provide happiness for them. I needed to only find peace and acceptance of myself. It was their responsibility to do the same for themselves.

The process of discovering this was a lengthy one. It included four years of treatment with a wonderful therapist named Adele Hoss.

I had stopped seeing Jessica Day in the winter of 2002 because she had moved her practice to another city. Although we tried to see another counselor, we didn't connect with him at all, and all of us just stopped going.

On my 49th birthday, on July 31st, 2004 – in a state of serious depression, and a feeling that I simply could not go on living the way I had been, I called my insurance provider, and finally found Adele.

I began seeing her on a regular basis – weekly, in fact for about a year and a half. At first I didn't tell Sam. He had already warned me (loudly) that I wasn't in need of therapy. He told me is would be a misuse of funds. I knew it wasn't a waste, but didn't want to fight with him about it. And when I first started going to see Adele, let's face it; I was still terrified of my husband's temper. It was one of the reasons I needed to go...

I had other issues in my life that were getting the best of me as well: financially, emotionally, vocationally, and personally. I felt out of control. I felt unable to cope.

Adele helped me to work through those issues. It was a long and painful process in many ways. In fact, for the first year I usually felt like things were worse instead of better. I had stuffed the closet of my emotional life so full that there simply wasn't any more room! Once I began pulling things out, I saw them, remembered them, and felt them again.

Moving into the second year I began to understand myself much more clearly. Adele was patient, honest, and understanding. Perhaps more than anything though, she validated me. She validated my experiences and my feelings. I believe that this was the reason my healing was possible.

After the first year and a half I began seeing her every other week, and eventually once every three weeks. Pulling the "stuff" out of my personal closet was difficult. Sorting through these things was very painful. Eventually, though, I learned to throw some things away, and keep only what I felt was necessary. My closet was neat and orderly. My mind was clear. My heart – though scarred – would survive. I felt strong, and unafraid. I saw my own reactions more clearly. I felt capable. I knew my own value. I was able to look in the mirror and see an amazing, tough, caring, and compassionate woman who knew how to love. I no longer allowed my husband to control my feelings. I was able to intelligently stand up for myself with other adults I had to come into contact with. Even my teaching skills were cultivated and expressed superiorly.

With all that I was now aware of, though, it was still not enough to release me from my some of my rescuing ways. I understood them – but I didn't really completely stop them (at least not when it came to my children). I saw them, but I still hadn't really learned how to say "no."

FIFTY-SIX

One month after Conner had gone to Bay Run the second time he called to let me know that he was going to go to a halfway house in Jacksonville, RI. "New Roads" halfway house was on Main Street. The main purpose of a halfway house is to provide daily instruction and practice in the development of positive life goals and responsibilities. It is a structured and supportive environment that empowers a patient to become successful in the transition from drug abuse.

I can't explain how happy I was that Conner had made the decision to continue his rehabilitation in an organized way. He left for Jacksonville on the 22nd of June.

It was the first summer I hadn't spent with my son, but it was for all the right reasons. I knew he was out of harm's way. I knew he was taking control of his disease.

The next 3-½ months were wonderful. I was still helping to pay his bills since he couldn't have a job while in extended care. I was still sending him a little money for cigarettes and a soda once in a while. Eventually, when it was permitted, I even bought him a *TracFone*.[39] I felt encouraged that he was on the right road, and I wanted to support his positive choices as much as I could.

---

[39] TracFone Wireless, Inc. All Rights Reserved.

By mid-August Conner had found a job with NNC Financial Systems. He was only making $8.00 an hour, but he was working full-time. He was learning to become responsible. I was very proud of him.

On October 8th, 2008 Conner moved out of New Roads, and into his own apartment in Georgetown (a city-suburb of Jacksonville). The apartment was small – two rooms, and a bath, but it was his.

We all helped him move. His sister, Sydney, gave him some furniture. I purchased a few things. Sam & I had delivered his car to him just a week before. It was wonderful to see him in his own place, holding down a job, and feeling so carefully confident.

For the first few months after Conner left New Roads he experienced a few disappointments – car troubles, budgeting difficulties – but he seemed content and more self-assured. Sometimes I became frustrated with his poor financial choices, but I was happy that he was clean. He was going to a meeting every day that he could, and by December he was heading the Friday night meetings.

I began to picture him as a drug abuse counselor. His sensitivities, his spirituality, his intelligence, and experience all seemed to point toward a future in assisting other addicts to stay clean.

If that kind of thing is meant to be, though, it isn't meant to happen quite yet.

FIFTY-SEVEN

"The brick walls are there for a reason. They're not there to keep us out. The brick walls are there to give us a chance to show how badly we want something."

-Randy Pausch

Conner hit a brick wall in January of 2008.

Even effectively treated people with addictions will confront unexpected situations after they leave a treatment program. This situation may produce intense periods of craving to drugs. Lapse, defined as re-use of drugs at least once following treatment, occurs in at least 50% of those who complete treatment. The most dangerous period for lapse is the first 3-6 months after completion of formal treatment. Relapse, defined as return to excessive or problematic use, is less common, occurring in approximately 20-30% of those who complete formal care in the prior year.[40]

Almost one year to the date (January 20th) Conner decided that it was "okay" to have a drink. He went out with some friends after work on a Friday night (to celebrate his birthday), and had a "few" drinks.

---

[40] A. Thomas McLellan, Ph.D., HBO Addiction, Treatment is Over. Now What if a Relapse Happens?

The following week, after a meeting, he smoked some weed.

Since he hadn't enjoyed the weed very much, the next week he drove to The Grazinglands Racetrack and Casino in Westmont County, Rhode Island and spent a couple hundred dollars of overtime money on gambling and more drinks.

Naturally, as we make these kinds of choices, we begin to feel negative feelings about ourselves. We know we are doing something that is going to harm us – something that is blatantly foolish! We feel guilty for having made a bad decision. We feel like a failure. We begin believing all the negative things that we have defined ourselves with for so many years. We forget our success. We only see our own collapse.

Then, in Conner's words, we just say, "Fuck It!"

The Jacksonville region, just 70 miles east of Portersville, is proud of its strong heritage, its strong work ethic and its strong sense of community. The city's autograph became "The Flood City" following two floods in 1963 and 1988. Most recently, the city has enjoyed the "The Friendly City" designation as Jacksonville, jarred by the demise of its industrial base in the 1980's, has reinvented itself as a result of efforts to economically diversify and enhance its image with industries based on new technologies and resource based tourism.

But Jacksonville is a small community. There's not that much "to do" in Jacksonville. Conner's excuse for getting high often became, "There's nothing to do to keep me busy." (He had quite a few excuses) Of course, it isn't the town's fault that so many addicts relapse. Relapse is part of the disease.

Multiple - and often interactive - factors can increase the likelihood of relapse. These are some of the commonly cited precursors:
- *Drug-related "reminder" cues (sights, sounds, smells, drug thoughts or drug dreams) tightly linked to use of the preferred drug(s) can trigger craving and drug seeking*
- *Negative mood states or stress*
- *Positive mood states or celebrations*
- *Sampling the drug itself, even in very small amounts*

The motivation to seek a drug, once triggered, can feel overwhelming and sometimes leads to very poor decision-making: the user will pursue the drug, despite potentially disastrous future negative consequences (and many past negative consequences).[41]

---

[41] Anna Rose Childress, Ph.D., HBO Addiction, What is Relapse?

Part of Conner's downfall came when a friend of his (from the halfway house) died. His friend had *MRSA*.[42]

It became apparent to Conner -at that point in his life - that sometimes working the program doesn't change the outcome. He had several friends who had relapsed. In fact, as time moved on, more and more of them seemed to be back on the street, robbing stores, and using drugs.

Perhaps one of the most difficult events he had to face was the disappearance of his sponsor. One day Jess was there, and the next day he was gone. No one knew what had happened to him, but rumor had it that he had also relapsed. Jess had guided Conner through quite a few moments of weakness - now it all seemed artificial in Conner's mind. In that particular moment he began to feel as if there were no such thing as "staying clean."

I honestly don't remember the exact conversation. You'd think I would, but I don't. One day Conner just decided to tell me that he had "slipped." He told me about the drinking, the weed, and the gambling.

I knew he had been having trouble. For one thing, his attitude seemed different. He was

---

[42] Methicillin-resistant Staphylococcus aureus (MRSA) is a bacterium that causes infections in different parts of the body. It's tougher to treat than most strains of staphylococcus aureas – or staph – because it's resistant to some commonly used antibiotics.

downhearted so much more often these days. He had started questioning things too – things like: his own future – his ability to get a "real" job or have a "real" relationship. He talked about his Hepatitis C, and how he wouldn't live to be 50 years old. He worried about his arthritis, and said that if he wasn't dead, he'd surely be in a wheelchair... He often sounded depressed. And he spoke of all the people he knew that had relapsed – about how difficult it was to find anyone who didn't "party."

Then, sometime at the end of February he told me that he had done heroin again!

"Only once, Mom. I don't know why I did it. But I'm not going to do it again. I actually did it three times, but then I got sick, and had to call off work. I don't want to do that anymore."

I can't say that I felt frightened. He seemed to have sincerely figured out that heroin was not his "friend." He talked about how many people go out and do a little "research" when they're in recovery. He had been skipping meetings since mid-July, and told me that he had decided to get back to it.

I felt hopeful.

But I was still worried so I did what I do so well – I started to nag.

I thought that I might be able to inspire him with my spiritualistic philosophies.

I explained his addiction to him. I quoted medical studies. I gave him excuses. I told him it was okay – these things happen.

It's not a sign of failure. And it's not.

Despite the availability of many forms of effective treatment for addiction, the problem of relapse remains the major challenge to achieving sustained recovery. People trying to recover from drug abuse and addiction are often doing so with altered brains, strong drug-related memories and diminished impulse control. Accompanied by intense drug cravings, these brain changes can leave people vulnerable to relapse even after years of being abstinent. Relapse happens at rates similar to the relapse rates for other well-known chronic medical illnesses like diabetes, hypertension and asthma.

How is relapse to drug abuse similar to what happens with other chronic diseases?

- *Just as an asthma attack can be triggered by smoke, or a person with diabetes can have a reaction if they eat too much sugar, a drug addict can be triggered to return to drug abuse.*
- *With other chronic diseases, relapse serves as a signal for returning to treatment. The same response is just as necessary with drug addiction.*

- *As a chronic, recurring illness, addiction may require repeated treatments until abstinence is achieved. Like other diseases, drug addiction can be effectively treated and managed, leading to a healthy and productive life.*[43]

I actually thought I could keep him from shooting poison into his arm again. I believed that something I might say or do would suddenly become some kind of epiphany for him, and he'd suddenly stop having cravings – or at least, be able to fight them off with his newfound wisdom (that I had so cleverly provided)!

Every day I'd ask him if he were clean. I'd count down the days that he "said" he was clean. I'd tell him how proud I was of him.

A lot of the time he was clean.

A lot of the time he wasn't.

Relapse is a cardinal feature of addiction, and one of the most painful.

Most people who struggle with addiction will have one or more relapses - the return to drug use after a drug-free period - during their ongoing attempts to recover. This can be extremely

---

[43] Nora D. Volkow, M.D., HBO Addiction, Addiction and the Brain's Pleasure Pathway: Beyond Willpower

frustrating for patients and for families, as they have already experienced great pain.[44]

For the next six months Conner struggled with his addiction. He lost three jobs because of it. If he didn't have money for heroin, he didn't steal or sell things (like he had previously) so he was in a constant state of either euphoria or withdrawal. He was dope sick too many times to count. He tried to go back to meetings. He didn't go to very many. He tried to rehab himself dozens of times. The longest he was successful was three weeks.

And the whole time, not only did I keep his struggle to myself, but I also continued to badger him every day with questions about how long he was clean, and proposals on how he might stay that way.

Every day - week in, and week out - month after month: Are you clean? Here's what you need to do… This is why you're having problems…

After all, I am such an expert! And (naturally) I would be able to fix it (if he'd just cooperate)!!

I'm absolutely sure I was driving him crazy! He always told me that he "understood" why I kept asking, but it truly was ridiculous!

---

[44] Anna Rose Childress, Ph.D., HBO Addiction, What is Relapse?

I'm supremely certain I was driving myself crazy as well, and although there's a certain kind of normalcy to this kind of behavior (in this type of situation), what I was really doing was showing signs of withdrawal from his recovery.

I was so involved with his recovery I was unable to let him do it.

I wasn't giving him responsibility for it because I was too busy trying to save him.

Though often unrealized, help for codependency, alcohol and drug addiction should many times be a family affair. As people read through the addiction family roles presented they can often identify the person in their life who plays each role. Roles though present in situations without addiction often become more apparent when an addict is present. Members will unknowingly take on specific stereotypes that can many times be classified as:

- *The Addict.*
- *The Hero.*
- *The Mascot.*
- *The Lost Child.*
- *The Scapegoat.*
- *The Caretaker (Enabler).*

I was (quite obviously) the "Caretaker."

The Caretaker (Enabler) makes all the other roles possible. They try to keep everyone happy and the family in balance, void of the issue. They make excuses for all behaviors and actions. The Caretaker (Enabler) presents a situation without problems to the public.

The underlying feelings are inadequacy, fear, and helplessness.[45]

One day in July of 2009, after being clean for three full weeks (or so he told me), Conner decided to get high again.

He called his old "friend," Mike Petro, drove to Houston (a part of town where street drugs were easily available), and purchased ten bags of heroin.

Just after making the purchase, the lights from a police cruiser flashed in his rear view mirror.

Mike started trying to hide his gear.

"Mike, sit still!"

Too late – the police don't miss much.

Conner pulled his car over to the side of the road.

Just like on an episode of the television show "Cops,"[46] Conner was raising his hands, and

---

[45] Hopelinks.net, Family *Roles* In Addiction & Codependency

stepping from the car. He was patted down, and the car was searched.

I'm not sure what it takes to be hauled off to jail for possession, but I guess it takes more than ten bags of heroin and a syringe. Both Conner and Mike were told they would receive a summons in the mail to appear in court, and they drove away "free."

---

[46] http://www.cops.com/

FIFTY-EIGHT

Addiction is described as being abnormally tolerant to and dependent on something that is psychologically or physically habit-forming.[47]

Co-Dependency is described as a condition that results in a dysfunctional relationship between the codependent and other people. A codependent is addicted to helping someone.[48]

It's no wonder I have always been so codependent.[49]

---

[47] Definitions of **addiction** on the Web

[48] E.Home Fellowship, Help With Life, Codependency Test and Definition

[49] Co-dependents have low self-esteem and look for anything outside of themselves to make them feel better. They have good intentions. They try to take care of a person who is experiencing difficulty, but the caretaking becomes compulsive and defeating. Co-dependents often take on a martyr's role and become "benefactors" to an individual in need. A wife may cover for her alcoholic husband; a mother may make excuses for a truant child; or a father may "pull some strings" to keep his child from suffering the consequences of delinquent behavior. The problem is that these repeated rescue attempts allow the needy individual to continue on a destructive course and to become even more dependent on the unhealthy caretaking of the "benefactor." As this reliance increases, the co-dependent develops a sense of reward and satisfaction from "being needed." When the caretaking becomes compulsive, the co-dependent feels

My mother physically, verbally, and emotionally abused me. My stepfather sexually abused me. My sister emotionally betrayed and abandoned me. I felt left out and alone as a teenager.

The need I had to "fix" others was born in the need I thought I had to fix myself.

I married a man who was verbally and emotionally abusive – who had a preponderance to temper tantrums, and who controlled me (perhaps unwittingly since he had so many self-serving insecurities as well). His domination was only possible because I was so afraid of all the things I had learned to dread growing up.

I did not feel safe.

I felt alone.

I needed some kind of power and order in my world.

I needed to feel needed (loved), and upbeat about whom I was.

---

choiceless and helpless in the relationship, but is unable to break away from the cycle of behavior that causes it.   MHA, How Do Co-Dependent People Behave?

The maze of psychology that human beings traverse is truly remarkable! In my world though – there is so much more.

There is a deeply spiritual side to my nature that seems to overpower every intensely frightening thing that has ever happened to me. If adversity has an enemy, its name is Faith. And I'm jam-packed full of it!

For reasons that may well create another story someday, I believe that all things are necessary as we move through our lives. There are no "bad" things that happen to us – just what seem like unpleasant experiences. I believe that there is not only a good reason for the circumstances of our lives – there is a deep, meaningful purpose to them.

I accept as true that *Love is the answer.*[50] I believe that the good, the bad, the happy, the sad, the confusion and the clarity are all bringing us to a place where we might stand more securely in that elusive, divine part of ourselves which I believe to be "God."

The trials of my life have taught me that they are essential gifts from my own soul. I may react to them as human difficulties (since that's what they are externally) but I can embrace them as delightful spiritual dances that weave the light of love into my heart.

---

[50] John Denver

And with these very lovely convictions, I have always seen what was happening with Conner or with Sydney or with Kim or even with Sam as experiences of divinity.

Sometimes we get caught up in our own human feelings. It's not a bad thing. We need to grow from the pain as much as we need to delight in the joy.

But in that moment – when Conner told me that he had been pulled over for possession of heroin, and that he was going to have to go to court – a spiritual light bulb went off in my head!

WHAT have I been doing?

I can't change anything! No matter what I've done thus far - no matter how I've supported him - no matter how much I believe in him, I can't make him recover!

I can't do it for him.

Theoretically, and intellectually I already knew all of this. But in that one moment it was as if I were physically and emotionally standing right in the center of the thing. I felt it.

HE is in charge of HIS OWN recovery!

And in that moment of deep awareness, I began to take control of mine.

FIFTY-NINE

These are the original Twelve Steps as published by Alcoholics Anonymous:

1. We admitted we were powerless over alcohol—that our lives had become unmanageable.

2. Came to believe that a Power greater than ourselves could restore us to sanity.

3. Made a decision to turn our will and our lives over to the care of God as we understood Him.

4. Made a searching and fearless moral inventory of ourselves.

5. Admitted to God, to ourselves, and to another human being the exact nature of our wrongs.

6. Were entirely ready to have God remove all these defects of character.

7. Humbly asked Him to remove our shortcomings.

8. Made a list of all persons we had harmed, and became willing to make amends to them all.

9. Made direct amends to such people wherever possible, except when to do so would injure them or others.

10. Continued to take personal inventory and when we were wrong promptly admitted it.

11. Sought through prayer and meditation to improve our conscious contact with God as we understood Him, praying only for knowledge of His Will for us and the power to carry that out.

12. Having had a spiritual awakening as the result of these steps, we tried to carry this message to alcoholics, and to practice these principles in all our affairs.[51]

---

[51] Alcoholics Anonymous

SIXTY

It had been an incredible month since my epiphany! I felt a freedom I had never known. I was liberated from my son's addiction! It isn't that I cared any less; of course, it was that I was finally able to really release control of it. I felt emancipated! I worried less. I slept better. I was no longer addicted to my son's recovery...

Conner came down to Portersville on the weekend of August 2nd, 2009. He was coming for a visit – as he did quite often – but there was a dual purpose to the trip. He had to get his fingerprints taken, and be in court for Controlled Substance charges at 12:30pm on Monday, August 3rd.

For at least 3-4 weeks (knowing he was still using – knowing he was trying not to) I had stopped asking him if he was clean. I explained to him that I would no longer be trying to help him recover. I told him that it was his responsibility, and that no one could "help" him – he had to do it himself!

On that cold Monday afternoon he waited in the court room for the bailiff to call his name. He was frightened. Conner had never been in trouble with the law (though he had escaped by the skin of his teeth a couple of times). He was scared he was going to end up in jail.

Finally, they called him. He approached the bench. The judge asked him if he had a lawyer. Conner said that he didn't. The judge gave him a continuance and rescheduled Conner's hearing for October 2nd, and told him to call the Public Defender's office.

Conner left the courthouse, drove back to my house, and called the Cougar County Drug & Alcohol Center. He made an appointment for the next day. He wanted to get back into formal recovery.

A terrace nine stories high begins with a pile of earth.

-Lao-tzu

"I love you, Mom. I'll call you as soon as I'm allowed."

"I love you too, Conner. I'm very, very proud of you."

On Tuesday, August 4th, at 12:58pm Conner left for detox. At this writing that was only yesterday. He will be at Bay Run again for at least another 28 days.

I don't know what the outcome of this rehabilitation will be. I don't know if he'll find the strength to deal with hardship or pain without covering it over and self-medicating. I don't know if Conner will be able to stay clean. I know that he says he wants to.

I was once told that an addict needs to want to be clean and sober 100% of the time – not just some of the time. I don't know what it will take for Conner to get to 100%. But I do know that it's up to Conner. I care about his sobriety more than I can say. I love him more than I might ever be able to explain.

But his addiction and recovery is his to own, and his to manage.

As for me – I have learned a lot about myself through the experiences of my life (including Conner's addiction). I have come to recognize my own conditioned responses, reactions, and fears. I have come to find my own personal strength, grace and worth. I don't do things any longer to try to make someone else happy. I am kind because it is the right way to be – because we all want others to treat us the way we would treat ourselves – and it makes me happy.

I've learned to appreciate what my grandmother told me when I was younger, which was simple. When you were born, your life was like an empty vase. All of your life people put flowers in your vase. You should give the flowers back because you don't want to leave this earth with your vase full.

-Irma P. Hall

I am learning (through the benevolence of a couple of good friends) what healthy relationships really are. All of my personal interactions are evolving, in fact. I find comfort in what I know to be true. I hope my family and friends are happy, but I know now that I cannot bring that to them. I cannot do anything to bring about their well-being. I can only love them.

And I can love myself.

To dream of the person you would like to be is to waste the person you are.

-Kurt Cobain

SIXTY-ONE

God grant me the Serenity to accept the things I cannot change,
The Courage to change the things I can,
And the Wisdom to know the difference.[52]

This is not a story about my son's addiction.

It's not a story about any of the other relationships or events in my life.

However, these things have been sustained, sometimes frightful catalysts for my own personal and spiritual autonomy.

This is a story of hope. It's a story about tender detachment. It's a story of love.

It's the story about my recovery from son's addiction.

There are reasons we sit still, and reasons we run.

I am finally learning how to walk.

---

[52] The **Serenity Prayer** is the common name for an originally untitled prayer, most commonly attributed to the theologian Reinhold Niebuhr. The prayer has been adopted by Alcoholics Anonymous and other twelve-step programs.

Conner's Epilogue
CHASING THE DRAGON
-Conner Jobes

I have always envisioned myself as a knight in arms - yet whom can I save now when I can't seem to save myself? It's an age-old myth - one single man against a dragon. Though the dragon, in this case, lay burrowed within me. Even now I can feel its uncoiled wrath burning in my gut. It is enraged for I have withdrawn in surrender. It calls to me in its silky, poisonous voice, *"Imagine the glory if you can beat me down. Imagine the fame if you can smite me. Women will lust for you! Men will lust to be you! Even in the battle there are moments of elation; are there not?"*

As its serpentine voice echoes coldly from the craggy recesses of the cave in my heart I think back to the war I have waged.

Trolls had I slain - ogres and demons, but never had I chased down the dragon. In those days my sword shone like the rays of the sun. Eventually, I came to a desolate land wasted by the great wyrm: the dragon. The people there were sickly, weak and thin from spending their lives in conflict with the beast. Even the children were born to suffering. They peered at me with fearful, bloodshot eyes from their shanties and hovels. Slowly, a whisper rose and followed after me on the bitter breeze: *"A knight comes! Does his armor not shine like the stars? Behold his steed – pale as the moon!*

Perhaps he can withstand the furnace of the dragon's fury!"

My courage was bolstered by the words of those broken people and I rode onward without rest. Yet another voice came to me from the village from an old man - weatherworn, and rotting on his feet, *"No one can dance with the dragon and claim victory. This man is no different. Were we not all once swift, proud, and strong? He cannot take the dragon's treasure. See if his head is held so high when he comes again – if he comes again at all."*

I turned my horse to destroy who had spoken and met the elderly man's eyes. I saw wisdom there and profound sadness. A part of me balked there but pride was stronger so I turned away and continued toward the rusty, brown mountain in the distance. I traveled across that land for some time. The strength of the dragon amazed me. That one entity could blight such a wide radius of land was uncanny.

Eventually the land began to ripple in little hillocks. It was upon that first rise that I met someone amazing. It was also my last chance to turn back, though I didn't know it.

A young lady stood upon that hill looking back the way I had come. She was breathtaking with hair of spun gold and the kind of brown doe eyes that men sing of. For a moment I thought that perhaps she was a dream, and I nearly passed her by. Then she spoke with the sweet softness of an angel's wing, *"It is lovely, is it not, Sir Knight?"*

I dismounted and looked where she was looking. Beyond the brown and dusty plain through which I had just passed, the sun was descending behind forested hills. It *did* work at my heart but the dragon was on my mind still.

"That it is, Lady. Why do you dwell so close to the dragon?"

She looked at me up and down, and then smiled in a knowing way. Her beauty struck me. She laughed, and then spoke, *"You are young and brave, Sir Knight. I suppose you are chasing the dragon that lives in yonder dire mountain?"*

When I nodded she continued. *"I am tired of this wasted realm. There are finer lands than this where perhaps I might find joy. It is not an easy journey but I will go. There is nothing but sorrow in the dragon's shadow, Sir Knight. You can come with me if you wish."*

I looked into her eyes and my will almost hearkened unto her. I had never imagined a woman as fine would ask for my company. Unfortunately I let my pride rule again. I rue that turn of my heart to his hour, but thus did I answer her, *"Nay, Lady. I cannot. Though it wounds me to do so, I must face the dragon. I feel as though this path has been chosen for me. I must test myself, and if fate be with me, I will destroy this menace."*

She looked away from me and her face grew grave. Indeed, it seemed she was near to tears. It confused me and somehow served to harden my resolve. I then could not follow to where she was going. She nodded and answered before she walked away, "*I thought your heart might feel that way. Do what you must. You are like the people of the valley that choke upon the dragon's stench – yet they stay because of its might. They know nothing else and its magic has laid hold of them. Sadly, the population in the valley grows daily for they worship the beast even as they fear it. I pray that the road you walk leads to no ill end. When you have finished with the dragon, if you can withstand its rage, look for me by my name. It is Serenity. Luck be with you, Sir Knight. You will need it.*"

I watched her walk away and almost called out to her. Yet, I had to let her go and hope that perhaps I would see her again. Thus, I continued my quest even to the mouth of the dragon's lair with fear and doubt now heavy in my mind. Rage and pride drove me onward until I stood with conviction at the devil's door.

The cave opened like a ravenous mouth in the face of the rock. From within came a golden brown glow like muted fire. I dismounted my horse for the last time and entered into the dragon's house. The walls were slimy and the floor of the cavern was strewn with discarded weapons. The remains of the slain were all about me and an icy chill gripped my chest. I drew my sword and brought my shield to bear in front of me. I knew that at any moment I would come upon the dragon.

As my eyes adjusted to the dim interior I saw that the chamber vaulted upward until it disappeared into the void. It was also wide – probably fifty yards across. In the center of the room was a pile of gold, gems, crystals and other bits of treasure. Some of it seemed old - older than I could imagine - in styles I had never seen.

It was upon this hoard that the dragon lounged. It would be fallacious of me to claim that the dragon was not majestic. The way it lazily raised its head from that pillow of riches was truly unthinkable. It fixed me with eyes of deep emerald. I was surprised to see that it was not red in color as the stories always said. It was light brown – almost tan. It chuckled, and thin streamers of smoke rose from its nostrils like floating snakes. Slime oozed from between its sword teeth as it spoke to me, *"Well met, son of man! Have you come to slay me and lay claim to the treasure? I am eternal! The only one of my kind! Greater men than you have been but a midday snack for my bottomless hunger! But you know this, surely you saw my thralls in the valley. Yes, and by the doubt in your eyes, you have seen that sneaky harlot, Serenity."*

I felt anger and fear at the same time. Also, from within me, I felt the ecstasy of the coming battle. In those days I lived for that kind of elation, and believed that I resided safely in the metal skin of my armor.

How suddenly things change. I did not dignify the dragon with an answer. Instead, I assaulted the beast. The first time I attacked it, I ran in with a confidence I had never felt before because rather than chasing the dragon, I was confronting it. I had a clarity I had been missing for years. Unfortunately my advance was defeated before it had even begun. My mighty strike rebounded immediately from its hide leaving only a tiny scratch on the pearly brown scales.

I lifted my shield just as the dragon released its hellfire breath. The force of the blast propelled me backwards – off of my feet – and knocked my shield, still flaming from my hands. I quickly discarded my helmet as well for the dragon fire was sticky and threatened to melt through. The dragon laughed belching forth great clouds of acrid smoke.

"Is this how you will destroy me little knight? Your sword is neither as long nor as sharp as my tooth. Come again! I have not had so much fun in a long time."

I took my broadsword in both hands, drew a deep breath to calm myself and replied, *"Even a tiny bee may kill a man if his venom is venomous enough, and that man be allergic. Perhaps, dragon, I am your allergy. Let my sword sting you and see if you boast so boldly!"*

The dragon's grin was horrific - a mess of black gums and green slime. I approached cautiously with my sword tip pointed menacingly at the dragon's throat. I circled to the left always facing the dragon. The beast merely grinned at me but I was not shaken. Then with a speed and grace I would have thought impossible for a creature so large, the dragon struck out with one ponderously huge paw. I dropped to my knees, reacting out of instinct alone, and I swept my sword up over my head. The dragon drew its own limb across my glittering steel and a deep gash was opened in the pad on its paw. Black, boiling blood erupted from the wound to hit the cold, stone floor and sizzle. The beast's eyes opened wide in alarm and it threw its head back, roaring in pain. A volcano of fire and smoke spewed from the dragon's throat. So much ash rained down that I had to squint my eyes to see through the tears. The dragon retaliated with its long, barbed tail striking the left side of my body with such force that I nearly collapsed. I landed on the ground in a heap of bent steel and broken confidence.

I could not rise immediately from my fall. The dragon's tail had been barbed and had penetrated my steel plant with little trouble. I removed the armor from my upper body with much struggle, and found that I had been wounded badly in my left arm. My back also had a shallow puncture. My blood was warm and I gritted my teeth against the pain as I rose to my feet. I felt a deep and paralyzing fear grip me. It was like sheets of ice water rushing over my body. I could not win. If I tried to run, I reasoned that the dragon would take flight and chase me down.

"What would escape prove for you little Knight? Don't you think the same would eat at you? Come and nourish me with your soul."

I knew then what type of enemy I faced. It seemed that the dragon had read my mind. I decided that only speed and wits could help me to beat this foe, so I removed my armor completely until I stood naked and in bare feet before him. The dragon waited and watched me smugly. Then before I had truly recovered, the dragon's tail came whipping out again. This time I was able to leap over the horned bars of its tail.

That was when I saw the loose scale. It was upon the dragon's underbelly, slightly eroded and lifted up from the ones beside it. A weak point, right before my eyes! When I landed, I moved quickly, plunging the sword into the discolored cavity with both hands. Hot blood exploded outward, scalding my arms, but I didn't let up. The dragon was howling in an eerie high-pitched way.

The more I fought, it seemed, the stronger the dragon became. I dove as it lashed out at me again with its claws. One lethal talon tore into my right leg but I was not gravely injured. My sword was stuck fast in the dragon's midsection, halfway up to its hilt. I pursued this avenue again running full force into the sword, pushing it in a few inches further. The creature writhed in pain and rage. I felt a clawed hand wrap around my middle and realized I was doomed if I could not get away. The dragon lifted me and bit my arm off some six inches above my wrist. The pain was incredible! Then I was flung like a pebble, some twenty feet, to collide with a stone wall.

My head swam and I was bleeding from many wounds. I understood that to engage the dragon again would surely be my death. Why not? I thought to myself - it would be an honorable death. But then I began to realize that something else was in store for me.

I thought of Serenity, the beautiful lady by the wasted plains. It is only for the desire of that lady that I still live. Then I saw something then that made up my mind. The dragon, although menacing and strong, had tiny, stunted wings that were more bone than anything else. Years of no use had made those appendages worthless. The dragon's body was bloated and fat. It looked as though the creature could not chase me if I wanted it to.

I lingered there, in utter pain and despair much longer than I should have. I knew that I could escape and live. However, part of me only wished to die in that place. I thought of what the people would say when I came back through the valley. Would they laugh? The stump of my arm hurt, and I could still feel my missing hand. Fortunately, it was not bleeding much; for the dragon's hot mouth had instantly cauterized the wound. I think the beast truly knew my thoughts, because for a moment I saw uncertainty in its terrible green eyes.

"You can leave, child, but know this: you will always wish you stayed. My power lies upon you now. You will remember the thrill of our conflict. You will know that you do not deserve life. Behold, I have taken a piece of you and I do not speak of your hand. Part of your heart will know that I defeated you, and you shall despair. My shadow will haunt you and you will wish to return. You are the type of man who cannot admit he has lost, and so your pride will bring you back."

After the dragon spoke, I stared at it for a moment. I digested its words and knew that, partially at least, they could be true. Yet, my mind had been made up. I wanted to live. So without answering the dragon, I turned and left the cavern. Its evil held onto me but I walked onward in spite of it. My final walk through that cavern was very difficult. I felt strongly that I must prove myself or die. Then I thought of the people in that valley trapped in the dragon's shadow. Perhaps I could help free them, and in turn help myself.

Now I stand outside of the cave that glows with the hellish light. The dragon's voice still echoes but I have chosen to ignore it. Before me the land looks new and amazing. Perhaps it was some work of the Gods that gave me this second chance. I know that if the choice was mine alone, I would be dead now.

Night has fallen and the moon rides in its cloudy cradle above me. However, beyond the dusty darkness of the valley below I know there are lands of forested plenty. I must face the shadow of the dragon and escape his realm if I am ever to redeem myself.

In some way, although he wounded me greatly, I will always have my time with the dragon in my heart. Somehow the dragon was truly my best friend. Perhaps if I had never faced it, I would still be walking a path of false pride and senseless violence. Perhaps that life might even have killed me.

I will never know unless, through some failing of my own resolve, I return to the darkness from whence I came. For today – I set my sights forward to face the coming struggle in the valley, and maybe, in some distant day, I will find Serenity.

The End?

Anne's Epilogue

It has been nearly a year since I wrote the final words of my story. So many things have changed!

My son, Conner, is clean now a little over ten months. He has a job, an apartment and a girlfriend. He is doing his best – struggling with "normal" struggles these days and although there is so much more to adjust to outside of his active addiction there is much more to be grateful for. Naturally, I haven't fooled myself into thinking that he's "cured." There is, unfortunately, no cure for addiction. But this time around he seems to have figured out what he really wants and he's certainly put in the right time, attitude and effort to make it happen. I have faith in him. I'm very proud of the man he is becoming.

After leaving rehab, Conner went to a halfway house for a little over three months. Then for four months after that, he followed through with outpatient care and two N.A. meetings a day. Since getting a full-time job and his own place, he has been going to meetings, doing his step work, working with his sponsor and recognizing that life – though challenging sometimes – is the better of two evils.

My story, conversely, is just as incredible!

I found strength within my epiphany with Conner that I could never have imagined before.

My attitude is more self-assured. I'm simply not afraid any longer.

My relationship with Sam has become more balanced and enjoyable because I now own self-respect. We get along so much better, in fact, that I see an enormous change in Sam as well. Both of us enjoy our lives together much more than we ever have. This is possible because it is truer than it's ever been.

At work I stand more strongly in what I know to be true – my own values, morals and talents are appreciated and utilized more because I am aware of them.

Conner and I still need to work on our codependence. We're both aware of the habits we've weaved into our relationship. We both know they're not healthy. We are both actively attempting to have an improved rapport – two adults who don't take advantage of or try to save one another. It's harder than it seems. We are so deeply conditioned to act a certain way with one another. But we continue to patiently strengthen each other.

Looking back on my experiences, I know that I have learned a great deal about love – but mostly – about loving myself. I have learned to forgive my loved ones for the choices they've made. I have learned to forgive myself for the sometimes preposterous things I've done. I have come to a newer and sweeter understanding and an inalienable faith in who I am and what my worth is in this life.

I've often heard it said, "If we fail to resolve our past, we are destined to repeat it."

Until very recently I was only aware of the certainty of this statement superficially.
But replicated behavior shows itself in many forms.

As we travel through life, and become more aware of our own actions - if we are wise enough to observe them, and honest enough with ourselves to face them – we see more than the façade of the things that "happen to us, "what people "do to us" or "make us do," and become aware of our own accountability in the destiny we live.

I have found it takes a courageous heart to peruse truth – to see our own weaknesses, and to step beyond them into forgiveness.

Forgiveness is much more than forgiving someone for doing something hurtful to you, for breaking your heart or for betraying your trust.

Forgiveness is more than forgiving the world for your circumstances.

Forgiveness is nothing more than forgiving yourself.

It is in that moment of absolution – that defining moment – that we begin to resolve our past, and rewrite providence.

COMING SOON
Anne Jobes' next novel:
Love Is What's Left

Preview:

INTRODUCTION

I looked into his dark brown eyes. They had become a restful, safe place to me. I hoped he might *really* understand how much he could trust his heart to me.

"No matter how big or small; no matter near or far – all you need to do is ask…"

He didn't reply.

I wasn't sure he knew how.

He looked deeply into my eyes. It was as if he was trying to really grasp what I had said – what I actually meant – trying to believe me, trying to trust himself to trust me.

We were sitting in the back seat of his car. Well, he was sitting – I was leaning across his lap. My arms were around his neck; his arms were holding me close.

"I mean it," I said. I looked at him lovingly. "Do you understand?"

A moment of stillness passed between us – our eyes were locked on one another's; our bodies were clinging to each other.

He bent his face toward mine, and kissed me. His lips parted. His tongue caressed mine. There was nothing I'd rather do than stay in his arms forever.

But it was almost time to say good-bye again. And I never knew if there would ever be another "hello."

Read Anne's other books:

Spirits of the Heart
Volume One

Spirits of the Heart
Volume Two

Spirits of the Heart
Volume Three

Of Light and Sound

Journey of the Heart
Volume One

Journey of the Heart
Volume Two

Melancholy Moments

Resources

HBO – Addiction: Why Can't They Just Stop?
http://www.hbo.com/addiction/

Narcotics Anonymous:
http://www.na.org/

Naranon – Support for families and loved ones of substance abuse users:
http://www.naranon.com/home.html

Made in the USA
Lexington, KY
08 January 2010